No! I Can't Afford It

Irwin B. Meisel, CLU

THE NATIONAL UNDERWRITER COMPANY
420 EAST FOURTH STREET
CINCINNATI, OHIO 45202

Second Printing, May 1985

420 East Fourth Street
Cincinnati, Ohio 45202

Library of Congress Catalog Number 81-80557
International Standard Book Number 0-87218-016-6

Printed in the United States of America

Dedication

To all the suspects, prospects, policyholders, and clients who have said "No" in all varieties from plain vanilla ("I can't afford it") to mintberry backswirl ("My son is studying to be a doctor and he's co-signing a note for me to open a motel"). Incidentally, I really heard that last one.

To my creditors who wouldn't take "No" for an answer and forced me to get more people to say "Yes".

To Harvey Brode, CLU, who actually convinced me to take my hand out of my pocket and say "Yes" to taking pen in hand and writing down these thoughts.

To all the salespeople who have used, worked, reworked, said, written, and conveyed some of these ideas and answers to objections. We've all said "No" to originality and "Yes" to plagiarism. If, in reading this book, you can truly say that one of these ideas actually originated with you and wasn't assimilated from some other source, call me and I'll refund the price you paid for the book. I always wanted to meet the real author of some of our standard or exotic ideas. As Harry Truman said, "There is nothing new in history except that which you haven't read." At the same time, I'll footnote those ideas that are original with me.

To Steven J. Radom and he knows why.

To my daughters Bonnie, Leslie, Shelley, and Dori who said "Yes" to the baton lessons, band trips, being beautiful girls, new dresses, college, big weddings, Thunderbirds, braces at age 19, contacts, and all the reaching, stretching ideas that make us grow. I had to say "No" to the lazy bug downtown so I could say "Yes" uptown to them.

To my wife Sharon, who said, "Yes, I do" one time, and has not said "No" since.

Contents

List of Illustrations

1

Salesmen and Other Living Creatures

"All the world loves a lover." But the same goodwill is not accorded to salesmen. We could not go so far as to say the world even dislikes salesmen. The little understood fact is that everyone is a salesman. Every working person in the world is selling a product or a service. Obviously, insurance agents sell a product, insurance. Milkmen sell milk. Furniture salesmen sell furniture. Grocers sell food. Computer repairmen sell the ability to fix computers, a service. Nurses sell their services for an hourly or weekly fee. Anyone who gets paid is either selling a product or a service.

Take this example: I was once doing an interview with a dentist. I was young in the business and the size of the case at that time was large for me. Frankly, I was in over my head for my experience. However, I was feeling comfortable and thought I was making progress. I was following a company-prepared sales track when suddenly the dentist said, "I couldn't do what you do, for anything." I replied, "I don't know what you mean." He responded with, "I couldn't sell people insurance." His attitude was demeaning and I could tell he was just tolerating me and had not been interested in what I had been saying. I felt terrible. He had made his point: salesmen were living creatures.

A sudden wave of genuineness rushed over me. I came out of my scared selling attitude and into a posture of honesty; an "I don't care what happens" attitude. I said, "Doctor, don't you realize that you are a salesman. Everyone is a salesman. You sell your ability to pull a tooth at $10 per tooth or your ability to fill a tooth at $6 per crack; but you're selling. Besides, I couldn't do what you do. I couldn't stick my finger in someone else's mouth." Sale!!

All the barriers came down. Anger reigned. His irreverent, baiting remarks were answered with my very truthful remarks; I couldn't actually put my fingers in someone else's mouth. The sincerity of this fact jumped from my eyes to his as he glowered at me. The sincerity of my return gaze transferred to everything I had previously said about my insurance proposal. He didn't know how to respond so he said, "OK, I'll take it but I'm not paying yearly; what's the quarterly premium?" He had now sold me on the fact that he was still the boss because he was directing the terms of this purchase and I wasn't making the sale according to my proposal.

Sammy Davis Jr. wrote a book entitled, *Yes I Can* which depicted the problems of a young black entertainer selling his talent to the established purchasers. His agonies struck home to me and I'm sure to everyone who read it. I'm certain that salesmen who read his book all empathized with him at the "No's" he had to take and the direct rebuffs and even violence he suffered. I believe he said, "Yes, I can" because everyone else was saying, "No, you can't." Ironically, isn't that where all salesmen lineup in the selling arena? It's almost like the coin toss at a football game when the referee says, "Blue has won the toss and will kick off; green has chosen the West goal to defend. Good luck, gentlemen." In this scenario, salesmen always kick off.

Picture this: The Prospect Team captains (they always need two) and the Salesman Team captain meet at the fifty yard line. The Prospect captain hasn't shaved, hasn't brushed his teeth, has his arms folded tightly, is looking down, is wearing a torn uniform which has a little blood on it showing where he demolished last week's opponent, and only mumbles when the referee speaks to him. Salesman captain, on the other hand, is cleanly shaven, holding his helmet under his arm, allowing us to see that his hair is neatly cut and combed, has brushed his teeth and even taken a swig of mouthwash in the locker room before coming onto the field, has his hand extended eagerly to the referee with the greeting, "Pleased to meet you, sir." He looks everyone in the eye with his head up, his uniform clean and the jersey that even has a pleat in it. He puts out his hand and suffers rejection as Prospect captain offers a wet, limp-wrist hand.

The coin is tossed and Salesman wins. "We'll receive," says Captain Salesman. "We'll defend," Captain Prospect says, unnecessarily. Incidentally, even if Prospect had won, the captain would have chosen to defend rather than kick off. Prospects always defend.

But when you think of it, even though prospects are always defensive, what is there about which to be defensive? What is the salesman actually trying to accomplish other than what the policyholder really wants himself? The two of them are truly going down different adjacent highways to get to the same place. One road is a toll road on which the fee is paid up front. The other is a *free* road where the *use* tax is levied insidiously by bonding, bureaucracy, bungling, bad repair and, sooner or later, a dead-end. The cost of the *free* road is always more than the *fair-share* road but it doesn't all have to be paid at once. Sometime the user himself doesn't have to pay; he leaves that for the passengers who were dependent upon him. The cost comes as surprises in the forms of expenses, debts, and taxes. In this event the toll could have paid the costs. Mathematically speaking its, **p = P**, (small **p** equals premiums, big **P** equals proceeds.) The other formula is **E − (e + d + t).** In this formula **E** is estate, **e** is expenses, **d** is debts, and **t** is taxes.

Why does the agent engender such evasive and defensive measures and attitudes on the part of the public? To my mind, there are a number of reasons. First, our product involves talking about death and most people dislike talking about that. Whether or not it's spoken, in a person's innermost feelings he doesn't want to think about death. He resents even the conversation with the insurance man. He doesn't necessarily disagree with the ideas but he's partially squeamish.

So we, as agents, soften the conversation with thoughts of retirement. Many times this proves to be not the most popular subject of the day. One has to get old to retire and most people don't want to think about growing old. Therefore, the salesman finds himself in another area of discomfort to the prospect.

Two negatives already and here comes a third: the premium. There is no question that every person wants exactly what we have to offer. Who can say "No" to security for family, security for self later, equity growth, collateral power, guaranteed loan interest rates, tax freedom, tax leverage, liquidity, and all the rest. One has to be nuts to dislike these things but you have to pay for them and that ain't the nicest thing. There is a cost either way but the premium method involves cost now, not later. Besides, later is such a long way off.

Regarding premium, the philosophy is the microscopic view of the big picture, the life insurance. The fact is that it has to be sold; it will never be bought. That's how it is with most things that are good for you. Candy is bought, diets are sold. Cigarettes are bought; stopping has to be sold. Ask a smoker why he started and he'll tell you he was thirteen years old and he wanted to prove he was "a man." Ask him why he's stopping and he'll tell you he is forty years old and he wants to prove he's "a man." Booze is bought; the cures are sold. Generally, religion is considered to be a good thing but it, too, has to be sold. Consider the last two items, booze and religion.

The doors of a church or synagogue are open perpetually. But I said the religion has to be sold. Not only does it have to be sold, it has to be sugar-coated, spoon-served, and force-fed. How do we get people into houses of worship? We sell them into them. We have a mens' club, ladies' club, choir, teen clubs, potluck dinners, dances, socials, and the most religious gathering of all—BINGO. Drive by some churches and see the Wednesday night bingo advertisement in a sign as sturdy and ornate as the name of the institution.

On the other hand, the local beer store does no advertising. There are few items in there that will do you any good. Maybe milk and juices are the only things. Cigarettes are not only bad but carry an ominous health warning on the package. We know the alcohol doesn't do much good, unless you're a stockholder of one of the companies. Candy isn't the greatest food. Potato chips and other snack foods contain salt and oils that will add nothing to nutrition.

When the walls of the beer store need painting or a general cleanup is needed, no money is spent on paint or materials. It's simple to contact one of the pop companies or candy companies and ask if they would like to place their new advertisements or signs in your store. In fact, if the owner lets it be known there is space available, he could start a bidding war and even get paid for allowing the space. Therefore, the corner pop store doesn't have to do much more than Mt. Everest, just be there.

So we have two institutions, one good for you and the other bad for you. One beckons you with wholesome family togetherness and the other seduces you with dangerous lures. I have never taken count, but I'd bet that more people go through the broken screen door of the corner beer store than through the double doors of the most architecturally beautiful cathedral, temple, or synagogue standing, including Saturday or Sunday when the attraction is only worship. Probably diet pop has swung the tills in favor of the quick-stop joints by 20 to 1 or more.

To my mind, one of the biggest negatives is the conscience of the prospective buyer. Let's say you have done everything right. You prospected by referral, you set up the appointment just where and how you wanted it, you conducted a great interview, you combatted the objectionable thoughts about dying and getting old, the client can afford the premium, but somehow there is a stall. He's objecting hard, he's squirming. He's fighting you and you just can't figure out why.

I offer the reason of the conscience of the prospect. Sometimes, without even knowing it, we've done everything right; in fact, too right. We've been so perfect that the customer has no reason to object to anything. Yet he does. What's really going on here? Many times we may be so right that we back the man into a defensive corner where the only action he can take is surrender or say, "Uncle." What I mean by this is that we have taken the possibility of a choice out of him. We have made him feel guilty. We've blown right by his hot button and hit the cold water faucet.

He may be saying to himself, "I know this guy is right. I knew it before he came in but he's taking the choice right out of me. Now my wife is looking at me and thinking to herself that I'm a fool for not having done this before. This guy is not going to push me around in my own house. I should have done this years ago. I'm going to set up this insurance. I'm going to buy some. But if I do it right now, I'll be showing everyone that I was a dummy until now. So I've got to work this around so it looks like my idea and that I've had some plans of my own on my mind for some time. Yep! I'm going to do it but on my terms."

All of this has been said silently by the circuits in his stomach computer and now comes the printout as he opens his mouth to speak. "I think it's a good idea. I'll probably do it, but I want to think it over. When is my age-change time before the rates go up?"

I submit to you that a guilty conscience is one of the reasons that men are negative regarding the buying of life insurance. Two other ideas which I will only briefly mention but expand upon later are the intangible aspect and the postponable aspect.

We come back to the idea that insurance has to be sold and usually by Salesmen or Other Creatures.

"May I help you, Sir?" is what we hear when we walk into a store. I wonder, does the salesperson really mean it? Suppose you are in a sports store to compare features of one kind of ski over another and your only purpose is informational. When the clerk approaches you with, "May I help you?", does he really mean that or does he mean may he help himself? Most times, when you say you would like information or that you're only looking, the attitude will change to a quick brush-off. Answers range from, "That's not my department," "You'll have to come back when Mr. Smith is here," "We only carry what you see," to "I don't know," to many others that don't imply help. It is the odd occasion when we meet someone who is interested in helping and jumps in enthusiastically to fully enjoy explaining your questions and help you. When you come across one of these professionals, you'll move heaven and earth to buy from them when you're ready.

Insurance is the only product that personifies and magnifies the spirit of "helping." The product itself is designed to help today's problems as well as tomorrow's. The agent's service and the product come wrapped together in one package called a premium. The word premium itself really describes what an insured gets in the insurance deal. As a noun, premium connotes reward or prize. I think this is an excellent description of the amount the policyowner pays. It has to be considered a *reward* to pay a grossly amplified payment to the beneficiary of your choice. Here is another definition: the rate at which stocks, shares, or monies are valued over their nominal amount. There is no need for words such as *deposits, credits, debits,* etc. It seems the old guys who put the magic of mortality tables and compound interest together knew what they were doing when they came up with the word premium. When you think of it in terms such as I've mentioned above why attempt to improve on success. Premium will do very nicely, thank you.

And what a premium the policyowner gets. The guarantees today that whatever service he needs in the future he gets for the one stipend he pays, the premium. If the original agent leaves the business, dies, or is replaced, the insurance company will provide all the service necessary, be it tomorrow or a thousand tomorrows from now. If the insurance company fails, other companies will step in and guarantee the policy conditions. Loans, beneficiary changes, business assignments, disability waivers, all of these things are guaranteed now and forever in something called a premium. Fabulous, just fabulous!

After twenty-four years in the business, I still wonder why there is the prevailing attitude that insurance agents are "other creatures." With the type of benefits we offer we should be welcomed like Mandarins, but we know it just ain't so. That is why I've taken pen in hand: just to muse a little to myself on why the system works like it does and the reasons why the public's attitude changes so slowly. I cite an unoriginal quotation about the "man who dies and went to Hell and didn't notice the difference for six months because he was an insurance man." Truthfully, if one has the stuff to withstand the college education period of this business, be it four years or ten years, we most likely wouldn't change anything, although at certain downer moments we would wish to change everything.

The second reason I write this book is to pass along some ideas, phrases, and sales aids that have worked for me. I gear this mostly to the younger agent who may be in need of a mountaintop look at our peaks and valleys. For the experienced agent, have a humorous and piercing look at some of our drama-filled situations. Everybody take what you can and piggy-back on it to your heart's content and your client's benefit.

Here we go!

2

"That's Alotta Money"

In the previous chapter we touched on the subject of premiums. Let me devote some space to various thoughts by the clients, agents, and industry in general. All of us too frequently do cost and benefit type selling instead of needs selling, especially in this age of computerized illustrations. It is no problem to push a button on the machine and get it to kerchunk out four pounds of paper to illustrate everything all the actuaries know about policy rate ingredients. Every $10,000 policy illustration can have 14 columns, times 30 years, which equals 420 figures in lines and columns. Add to this the summary including interest-adjusted indices and you have a beautiful format which should sell itself. My point here is that we get too hung up on the cost and sometimes forget the problem and the solution. The clients work us into this position and if we're not careful we can get trapped into concentrating on the wrong thing.

Consider this actual situation and see if a few proper words put the case back into perspective. I had an interview in Saginaw, Michigan with three shareholders of a business. They came from three different cities where their chain of stores had operations. One was from Detroit, one from Lansing, and one from Saginaw. We had our meeting and it resulted in a stock redemption sale of $600,000. The applications were taken and I made arrangements to pick up the check from the Detroit shareholder's office, where the company offices were. The premium was $14,000.

I arrived at the office and met with Bill. There was great activity going on since it was around the tenth of the month and in this particular drug store business it was important to pay the bills promptly in order to get a two percent discount. There were two girls working in the outer office calculating the accounts payable. Over to one side of Bill's office was a temporary desk type arrangement so the bookkeeper could write checks and keep up with the extra help getting the bills ready.

Bill and I were a fair distance away from the bookkeeper and I don't think she was even paying attention to us. I turned the small talk off by saying, "Bill, let's take care of our business." His voice lowered to a whisper. "How much is it?" Since he whispered, I lowered my voice to an almost inaudible tone. "Fourteen thousand dollars."

"That's alotta money," he said even lower.

So I responded, keeping my voice level down, "Which, the $14,000 or the $600,000?"

He looked me in the eye and realized that was the bottom line of the conversation and he wasn't going to get all the reselling he was looking for unless I felt it was really necessary. I thought my question answering his question was perfectly in order and resold the entire need and verified the decision that all three shareholders had agreed upon the night before.

Suddenly, all the secret conversation stopped and he said to the bookkeeper, "Make me out a check for $14,000."

Bill neglected to ask me if it was deductible but if he had we would have been into an area that seems to be a source of problems for many insurance men. The simple fact is that buy-sell insurance is not deductible. There is a sound reason for this but we have to explain to the customer why it's to his advantage not to deduct.

Many years ago I learned the response that excludable was better than deductible. The reasoning here is that no deduction is allowed for the premium but the proceeds come back to the corporation income tax free. Once again, we have the principle of small **p** or big **P** being proceeds.

This next answer is one of the originals I referred to in the dedication. "Mr. Prospect, you bring up an interesting concept and you sure know your financing. We always have to be concerned about the lowest cost but listen to how the Government taxes this life insurance; you know they must collect taxes in every financial transaction. For whatever the reasoning is, they allow the full proceeds to come into the business tax free but for this they do not allow a deduction on the premiums you pay. Of course, you pay tax on the relatively small annual premium. Since we have to pay taxes anyway you would think the IRS would want to get it on the biggest end but that's not the way it works, so let's take advantage. I think you'll agree you don't want the premium deductible if they're going to tax the benefits. It would be terrible to think $100,000 is going to flow into the corporation but have it hit the tax filter first and not really know what is going to be available to complete the insured obligation."

Another answer is, "You can't deduct what you haven't spent or what doesn't depreciate. You really haven't spent anything when you pay a premium. On your balance sheet the most liquid asset shows up first. They should then be listed in descending order of liquidity. When the money is taken out of the *Cash* asset line, after the first year of the policy, the case value equity has to be carried somewhere so it is put on the line called *Cash Value of Officer's Life Insurance*. You can't deduct it because the only thing that has happened is that it has moved from one form of asset to another.

"Incidentally, since the cash loan or surrender value of the policy is as liquid as it is, which is only about six or seven days away, I feel it should be item number two on the asset ledger. Certainly it's more liquid than *Accounts Receivable* or *Notes Receivable* as an asset. In addition, someday the face amount of the policy is going to come flowing in as an asset so once again, assets to assets, dust to dust. No deduction!"

This idea, comparing premiums to proceeds, can be used for either term insurance or permanent insurance. The response regarding assets obviously doesn't work for term insurance. It applies only to permanent policies.

Sometimes I preface my remarks regarding the deductibility of premiums by asking the question, "Why do you want to deduct it?" Oftentimes, their responses will lead naturally into one of these answers: "I want the cheapest protection I can get." Or, "Isn't it to my advantage to deduct it?" On a rare occasion you'll find a business owner who *is* deducting his corporate insurance. It's illegal and most of them know it, although I'm sure some business owners have been told by some of us that they could deduct it. I repeat, it's illegal. If they get caught on an audit, they'll have to pay the tax and penalties on the amount deducted.

When you do spot someone deducting premiums illegally, tell him so. It won't hurt a prospective sale, especially if you're not the original agent. The truth will only raise his estimation of you and your knowledge. If he was doing it unwittingly he'll respect you for a proper explanation and add credence to the rest of your presentations. If the client is cheating on his taxes, he doesn't want to hear it from you. You won't make a new sale and the truth of the situation is that you don't want him for a client anyway. Your relationship will be short, if at all. In addition, you may eventually get hurt along with him.

Sometimes I lead into one of the above answers with the following example: "Term is a great idea when it fits, so let's talk about it. The question is whether or not you can really afford it. The cheapest term insurance available is airline insurance. You put $.50 in the slot and you have $12,500 of insurance for a three hour term or whatever is the period of the flight. Let's assume the flight is for three hours. There are eight, three hour periods in a day, so the premium for a full day in the air is eight times this measly $.50, or $4.00 a day. If you could arrange to stay in the air for a year, the annual premium would be $4.00 times 365 days or $1,460.

"Now a current, deflated half-copper U.S. half dollar isn't a lot of money in one coin, but it sure adds up if you want a full year's protection. You tell me if you think it's worth it. I repeat, I don't know if you can afford it.

"Buying term from any company is the same as putting $.50 in the slot. It adds up quickly and it gobbles the premium as quickly as a slot machine in Las Vegas. It pays off just as infrequently. All of the losers in Las Vegas casinos are just trying 'to get their money back.' Often you will hear them say, 'I just want to get even.' Do I really have to finish the story or do you know the gambler's syndrome? Ninety-nine percent of them don't get their money back. The odds are about the same for purchasers of term insurance. But if the policy expires before the insured does, he loses two things: the premiums paid and the face amount. I repeat, I'll sell you term insurance if you want it but I don't know if you can afford it. Look a little more closely at the permanent policy and let's see if it makes more sense for today but, more importantly, forever."

(This last example was another of those original ones.)

Chapter Three will be devoted to a few illustrations of term versus permanent but let's now devote some time to what many think is the cheapest way of buying insurance: rebating. The request for a rebate doesn't happen often but we know that it does happen. I've only had it happen to me a few times in twenty-four years but it's always been an embarassing situation. Mostimes, you don't know if the guy asking for the rebate is kidding or not. More often, he doesn't know if he's kidding or not. Sometimes he feels squeamish about asking. Sometimes he is dead serious, maybe thinking we are making too much money on his bestowing a sale on us. Sometimes he is a true chiseler. One time I had what I felt was a serious, honest request for a rebate. It came from an Indian doctor who came from a culture where haggling for price, rebates, refunds, and gifts were common.

Here are a couple of actual situations and the responses I used. Once, while I was at a synagogue dinner a man said to me, "Burt, is rebating prevalent in Michigan?" This question came out of nowhere and we certainly had no discussion that had anything to do with insurance. The long table was full with families, including two who were clients. All eyes turned to me for my answer; the scene was akin to the moment of truth on the witness stand. I asked, "Sy, where are you from and is it prevalent there?"

He wasn't as brave and mumbled to me, "I'm from Pennsylvania and I thought I heard about some of the people who do it."

I told him, "It's illegal in Michigan; I guess it goes on but I rebate." With this both my clients forgot their food and gazed hard at me.

"You do?" Sy said.

"Yes. I do. The commission rate is about fifty percent and you can have any part of that you want."

"I can?" Sy asked excitedly.

Now it seemed that everyone was staring at me. I answered, "Yes, on one condition."

"What's that?" Sy eagerly asked.

I responded, "Make me fifty percent of the beneficiary."

He seemed perplexed. "What good does it do my family to buy insurance from you?"

I calmly answered, "What good does it do my family to sell insurance to you?" Sy became quiet. My two clients relaxed and the topics of conversation changed.

Later in the evening, Sy cornered me and told me that I had embarrassed him. I wouldn't let him off the hook and equaled his remark by saying he had embarrassed me by even implying in public that I might be a party to rebating. I then asked what was his current interest in insurance. He said, "I have to make a business loan and the banker insists on debt insurance in my corporation." He told me that as soon as his loan was approved he would get the insurance from me because I showed him my protection of the integrity of my product and he wanted an agent who would protect his interests with the same vigor. He also indicated any rebate would not be worth the chance because an agent, who would cheat himself, wouldn't have too many qualms about cheating him also.

On another occasion, a prospect said to me, "You make a nice premium on this, don't you?"

I replied, "You mean commission, don't you, Mr. J______?"

He said, "Yes, we're paying you pretty good for this sale."

I could tell by his attitude that he was building up to ask for a rebate so I said, "Mr. J______, I do get paid pretty well for this deferred compensation insurance but I'm happy that my clients will always make more than I do. Also, in reality you don't pay me at all. There is no deviation in premium even if you could buy directly from the insurance company. Therefore, in this transaction you get two things: the policy and the services I have to offer. The insurance company actually pays me."

This handled the inquiring attitude very well and he was my client for many years. He died a few years ago and we paid a claim which was instrumental in providing cash when needed. His son is now insured with me and still runs the family business.

In another situation I handled a rebate request by asking for one for myself. Two shareholders, Teddie and Barry, were in my office to talk about the insurance to fund a buy-sell arrangement. Teddie was 58 and Barry was 40. We completed the applications, whereupon Teddie said to me, "Burt, you have made a nice commission on this deal and the ones on the other stores in the chain. You ought to take Barry over to Petrie Clothiers (a fine Detroit area shop) and buy him two or three suits."

I said, "Okay Teddie, that's a deal. When do you see Abe to have the buy-sell contract drafted?"

"Monday, why?"

"It's against the law to give trades or gifts on insurance purchases although I do it anyway. But I want to protect myself so I don't lose my license over any one deal. When you see Abe on Monday have him draft into the agreement that when Barry dies, the store will pay for five or six suits for me from the policy proceeds. After all, it will be no problem since that amount will be far greater than the premium now or even the commission now. That way, I'm protected.''

Teddie said, ''Forget it; I was kidding.''

I responded, ''But I'm serious. I don't mind doing what you said.''

Barry chimed in, ''He didn't mean it, Burt.'' It ended there with smiles and no hard feelings although I'm sure Teddie felt nothing ventured, nothing gained. These people and their other stores have purchased insurance many times since and we've never had a repeat of this issue.

On another occasion, I had a series of meetings with the corporation leaders of a meat provision company. The father was 74 years old and still active. Sons Bernie and Jory were in their 40's. We were designing a profit sharing plan and were working toward a January 31, 1974 deadline. One meeting had been postponed by them and we were running out of time. I had telephoned Bernie that afternoon to tell him that a corporate resolution and a bank deposit were needed. He was evasive on the phone and said he would call me back. He did call me at home that night.

He stammered a little as he said, ''I'm not asking for me but Dad and Jory want to know if there's any kickback from buying the plan. In our business it is common to give rebates to maitre d's and owners.''

I explained that I didn't do it.

He said he would call me back later. He did call about an hour later and said they had decided to set up the plan with their casualty man so all their insurance could be in one package. I told him I suspected they were getting a rebate and if I could prove it I would turn all of them over to the insurance commission. I also told him there were penalties on the corporation and shareholders, as well as the insurance agent. He tried to assure me that 74 year old Dad with all of his business savvy felt it was better and there really was no rebate.

Subsequently, I saw them at a social function. The sons tried to avoid me but the father thought he recognized me. I told him I had met with them the year before regarding the profit sharing plan. He said, ''Oh yes, you're the tax man.'' Later, after he had mingled and seen his sons he, too, was ashamed to look me in the eye. Was it really worth it to cheat?

The kicker is that on September second of that year ERISA was hatched and subsequently the rebating agent found himself in over his head and there were considerable problems with government agencies.

Summary: Sell the insurance that is the right plan for the right situation for the right premium and someday beneficiaries will say, "That's alotta money!"

3

Show Me!!

In Chapter Two I mentioned I would show some of the illustrations I use in presenting term insurance and permanent insurance. First off, let us all admit that term insurance has it's place. We all know what the place is and when the time is right for term insurance. The airline policy is a great example of proper use of term insurance. The three hour flight gets three hours of insurance; the four hour flight gets four hours of insurance, etc. Even a simple matter like throwing fifty cents in the slot for term insurance tells us a tremendous story about the *need* for insurance.

Our product most always takes us through the channels of, "I don't need it," through the straits of "What's cheapest?" to the island of "I can't afford it." But think of the dynamics of what's going on when John Traveler steps up to the slot machine to buy flight insurance. He's usually dressed in his best clothes since he's flying on business. He indicates to the world he is successful because he looks sharp and efficient, and he portrays an aura of worth because he's not afraid to proclaim to the world, in front of everybody, that he cares. He's going to take the time to buy protection for all those dependent upon him. Everyone is in such a hurry in an airport. But our man stopped to take care of his estate planning, publicly. What must be going on in the heads of the hundreds of fellow travelers passing by as they see him with his gold-tinged pen unashamedly saying, "I need it, I don't care what the cost is, and I can afford it."

This might seem like one insignificant transaction but think carefully what has happened. The machine has just closed a sale. The closing ratio is 1 out of 2,500 but the law of averages works here too. In addition, the machine only does one kind of interview. There are those of us who say we can't do a "canned" presentation. This robot just did a "machined" interview and made a close. It makes you wonder if one machine is painted nicer than the other or has more gears and printers on the inside or if the location is the only factor. But the machine demonstrated very clearly one thing and it did the simplest interview in the world. It said there was a need and it asked the public to buy.

It's all kind of stupid on the part of the purchaser because he is really indicating his thoughts of invincibility and immortality because he is now saying, "As long as I don't fly I don't need life insurance, but when I get in the air I'm removing something from my own control so I better insure. I sure do love Mary and the kids and two days after I'm back home and the policy comes in the mail, I'll show them how much I care. I'll tell them I did this for them. If I die, they'll file the policy and they'll know what a great guy I was." His thoughts continue as he fills out the punch card. "What should I do about the beneficiary? What was it that insurance man said about estate taxes and marital deduction, half for her and half to a trust? Decisions, decisions. I'll leave it all to her. After all, it's more than I had when I left the house. Boy, I feel good. I'm doing a good thing and all these people walking by me like me and respect me. Well, that's finished. Now I'll complete the rest of my business by getting the *Playboy* magazine and I'll relax."

Our big spender could have been less of a show-off by doing it all anonomously by checking the box only once with his charge card billing. Then he would have been more efficient because he bought more comprehensive term insurance, one that covers him for all flights in the future. All he has to do is charge the airline tickets and the computer will automatically bill him three dollars for maximum coverage. No agents, no physicals, no age changes, no fuss, no bother, no P.S. 58, no lawyers, no nothing. It's also no wonder so many of us have bad months at Christmas and New Years and other holiday times; it's peak travel times and everyone has just done his estate planning, the competition is tough. As an aside, I wonder what the grace period is if the traveller dies and next month's bill isn't paid on time or the check he wrote for last month's charges bounced, and the account were in arrears?

All of the above were humorous ways of looking at some of the approaches and propositions that do sell life insurance. Seriously, we all preach the gospel of a full-time pilot and that is full-time policies planned carefully with a competent flight instructor agent—you. But we must come back to the fact that people do indeed want life insurance. Otherwise, the machines would be unprofitable and would disappear from the airports. The machine stands by full-time. It never stops doing interviews and it closes by doing the simplest interview in the world—a one word appointment—**buy.**

I try in all of my selling to simplify the interviews and the proposals to the fewest but most effective words and ideas. I'm going to illustrate a few of these proposals designed for showing the difference between term insurance and permanent insurance.

In all of these situations the key is establishing and identifying the need. I do that first, then present a proposal that is designed to be simple, direct, and show the prospect what is the best method of obtaining the needed protection. It is designed to show him immediate costs and total costs along with ultimate guaranteed values.

Case #1

This first example goes back to December, 1975. The client owned a manufacturing firm and had done a tremendous job of getting together with his lawyer, accountant, banker, and insurance man. We all knew each other well and collaborated freely in setting up the client's personal, business, estate, and retirement planning. His 21 year old son had now completed work on his engineering degree and was coming into the business with his father, who owned 100% of the shares. Son, Bob, had worked in the plant for the past four years in all forms of labor. He had never been involved in management. The father's ultimate goal was to either gift, will, or sell the business to Bob. There were younger children involved so the father could not decide what was the best way to arrange his affairs with Bob. The dilemma was one of being too young and not yet wealthy enough to gift away too much of the estate.

A second problem was the nagging thought of reserving a part of the business for another son, thirteen, who may wish to come in later. A third problem was Bob's young age and the father's lack of confidence in making a buy-sell agreement with him right now.

But the common known factors were that Bob's future was in the

Illustration 3-1

Age 21 Bob R. $150,000

Year	Age	Increasing Premium	Level Premium	Decreasing Premium
1	21	$ 499.50	$ 1,152.00	$ 1,902.00
2	22	499.50	1,152.00	1,902.00
3	23	499.50	1,152.00	1,777.50
4	24	499.50	1,152.00	1,677.00
5	25	499.50	1,152.00	1,587.00
9	29	504.00	1,152.00	1,293.00
10	30	504.00	1,152.00	1,242.00
11	31	531.00	1,152.00	1,188.00
17	37	628.50	1,152.00	894.00
18	38	628.50	1,152.00	847.50
19	39	628.50	1,152.00	814.50
20	40	628.50	1,152.00	778.50
21	41	828.00	1,152.00	742.50
22	42	828.00	1,152.00	714.00
23	43	828.00	1,152.00	684.00
24	44	828.00	1,152.00	655.50

26	46	1,179.00	1,152.00	592.50
27	47	1,179.00	1,152.00	562.50
28	48	1,179.00	1,152.00	529.50
29	49	1,179.00	1,152.00	496.50
30	50	1,179.00	1,152.00	463.50
33	53	1,752.00	1,152.00	364.50
34	54	1,752.00	1,152.00	330.00
35	55	1,752.00	1,152.00	297.00
39	59	2,572.50	1,152.00	156.00
40	60	2,572.50	1,152.00	120.00
41	61	4,182.00	1,152.00	85.50
42	62	4,182.00	1,152.00	51.00
43	63	4,182.00	1,152.00	16.50
44	64	4,182.00	1,152.00	(CR)18.00
Totals @65		$59,605.50	$50,688.00	$34,324.50
Cash Values @ 65		$ 0.00	$89,095.00	$85,800.00

business and that the corporation would "always" want to do something for Bob. It appeared the only answer was a free-floating key man policy to guarantee insurability now and be available for assignment to specific needs later on. We, therefore, clearly agreed there was a need and the father said, "We'll want $150,000 of term insurance."

"I don't have the rates here now so I'll make a proposal and come back," I said. The most important word in our discussions was "always." To me "always" indicates permanence. But the father said "term." I thought about it for a long while, realizing if I prepared a full blown illustration showing a comparison of term versus permanent and investing the difference at 5% (in those days), I would confuse the clients who in the past had demonstrated a short attention span.

I decided to make an illustration showing only the progression of premiums and the accumulation of cash value at age 65. I decided to show five year renewable term, non-par, and participating ordinary life. The result is Illustration 3-1.

I believe people like things that are logical and simple. What could be more logical than one column of increasing premiums, one of level premiums, and one of decreasing premiums. So, that is the title I gave to the policies. Incidentally, I've since learned that if you give people a number of choices, they generally take one of the middle options. I don't know the reason but I've noticed that's how it works.

I did the interview in their office on the portable overhead projector so I could maintain control of attention. After we talked for a few minutes and I was satisfied the need was firmly reestablished, I flashed the illustration on the wall. The father said, "We'll take the increasing premium." I knew I was going to have to now start working, when Bob said, "Just a minute, Dad. Look at age 41; the decreasing premium is down to $742.50. The increasing premium is up to $828.00 and from then on costs more." Mind you, I haven't yet said one word since I put the acetate on the machine.

Bob continued, "If you were going to buy $150,000 today at your age, 47, anything would cost more than the $562.50 decreasing premium. Look at age 64. I don't have any more premiums and look at how much money we get back compared to what we pay. It comes out to a $51,000 gain. You always told me this business buys its machinery rather than leases it. It looks like we're just renting the insurance. I don't want to have to pay $4,182.00 when I'm 64." Bob said everything I would have said. His interview was going great; I would not have changed a word.

The father had to say something, so he said, "But Bob, we'll pay four times as much this first year."

Bob answered, "Burt, when does the cash value start?"

"After year one it starts going up by at least 80% of the second year's premium," I answered.

Bob said, "Dad, it looks to me like it's just one year's front money."

The kid made so much sense and he was absolutely right and sincere with pure logic. The father said, "You're right, we'll take the decreasing premium."

This is a very fine family with a close, friendly agent-client relationship and if the sale had been term insurance instead of permanent, for all the reasons the businessman knows better about his business than I do, that would have been fine. The conversion would have been made as soon as possible. The point here was the simplicity and directness of the proposal that caused the uncluttered mind of a 21 year old businessman to see the precise purpose of permanent over term insurance. Moral—**unclutter.**

CASE #2

Since 1975, I have been using simple variations of this original proposal, Illustration 3-1. Illustration 3-2, which I call "Gerald," is a reproduction of a January, 1980 case. As a result, all of my term-permanent proposals have come out as variations of the same theme but once again, why tamper with success. It's working for me. These illustrations are simple to make whether you do them yourself or an assistant does them for you. The only thing needed is the premium, whether you get that from a rate book or an expanded illustration and the values you want to show at the anticipated stopping point.

The facts of "Gerald" are these: I sold him an additional $50,000 term policy in 1976. He owned a Keogh plan through his small business, funded with a mutual fund. In 1975, we put some life insurance in the plan through the split-funding provision of the prototype document the fund had. The premium then was $1,200 yearly and amounted to about one-third of his annual contribution. Totally, he owned about

Illustration 3-2

Gerald

Comparison of Insurance Inside or Outside of Keogh Plan

Age 48 $50,000 Protection

	Increasing Premiums		Decreasing Premiums	
Year	Before Taxes	After Taxes	Before Taxes	After Taxes
1	$ 385.50	$ 539.70	$1,582.00	$949.20
2	564.00	789.60	1,561.00	936.60
3	564.00	789.60	1,527.00	916.20
4	564.00	789.60	1,496.00	897.60
5	564.00	789.60	1,464.00	878.40
6	564.00	789.60	1,431.00	858.60
7	902.50	1,263.50	1,402.00	841.20
8	902.50	1,263.50	1,372.00	823.20
9	902.50	1,263.50	1,343.00	805.80
10	902.50	1,263.50	1,311.00	786.60
11	902.50	1,263.50	1,278.00	766.80
12	1,404.00	1,965.60	1,246.00	747.60

13	1,404.00	1,965.60	1,130.00*	678.00
14	1,404.00	1,965.60	1,099.00	659.40
15	1,404.00	1,965.60	1,063.00	637.80
16	1,404.00	1,965.60	1,028.00	616.80
17	1,788.50	2,503.90*	994.00	596.40

Total Premiums Paid to 65 -	$31,137.10	Total Premiums Paid to 65 -	$13,396.20
Total Equity at 65	$ 0.00	Total Equity at 65	$18,718.00
Total Paid-up Insurance at age 65	$ 0.00	Total Paid-up Insurance at age 65	$28,250.00

*Waiver of Premium Benefit Ends

$150,000 of coverage. I felt he needed more insurance but he was convinced he didn't. I decided to concentrate on making the $50,000 conversion. During the interview, after my urging, he made his periodic promise that he was going to see his lawyer to get a will. I anticipated the objection to additional insurance so I prepared Illustration 3-2, thinking he was now contributing more to his Keogh plan and we could install more life insurance there.

This was exactly how it turned out. He was putting $7,500 yearly into the Keogh plan. The illustration in the "Before Taxes" column shows the term premium. The "After Taxes" column shows the premium, adding in 40% for income taxes. (I must admit my column headings were not clear. I could have worded them differently but I'm showing illustrations that actually worked and this one did, poor language notwithstanding.)

Under the "Decreasing Premiums" section, the "Before Taxes" column is the net premium for permanent insurance and the "After Taxes" column is subtracting a 40% tax bracket. He fought me on the idea of making the conversion into the HR 10 plan since he still felt permanent was more expensive than term. However, my simple columns and values at age 65 are tough to refute, especially "-0-" under "Equity" and "Paid-Up Insurance." The result of this meeting, which was held at his home with his wife present, was that he thought I had a good idea and would arrange a meeting with his lawyer to discuss this, along with wills and trusts. I told him I would agree to wait two days for him to call me with the date for the lawyer meeting or I would call him back and insist he make this conversion without legal consultation, since I was the only advisor he had. On the second day he hadn't called me so I called him. To my surprise, he did already have a date with the attorney.

He saw the attorney who set up a will and a trust, recommended he make the conversion of the "$50,000 Increasing Premium" policy into the HR 10 plan, and buy another $100,000 "Decreasing Premium" insurance.

CASE #3

In this instance, I had done an estate planning interview with the prospect in June, 1979. We could not complete the work because so much depended on what the client's father was going to do about his stock on retirement, between two and five years. Len wanted to check with the corporate attorney regarding certain plans the company had for him. I called him the first week of January, 1980. He told me his attorney recommended he buy $250,000 on a personal basis. He asked that I get a quote for the "cheapest" term available.

I made Illustrations 3-3 and 3-4. Column "Worst Conversion Options" was an extremely low cost company. The term was cheap and I did not include waiver of premium. Conversion to a permanent policy would not be a competitive buy. Therefore, I called it "Increasing Premium, Worst Conversion Options."

"Increasing Premium, Best Conversion Options" was yearly renewable term with a large mutual company. The rates included premium waiver and the ordinary policies on conversion would be most favorable.

"Decreasing Premium" was strictly ordinary life with premium waiver and premium reduction dividends.

"Decreasing Premium, Decreasing Insurance, $250,000 to $100,000" was permanent insurance of $100,000 with a $150,000 decreasing term rider.

On the interview I first gave Len Illustration 3-3 only. You will notice there is nothing on the sheet except the premiums to 65 and the cash values. Len looked it over as I said nothing. He said, "Column four looks the best."

I said, "You're right but did you notice the insurance decreases from $250,000 to $100,000?"

Len said, "Oh, then three looks better." I agreed. I then handed him Illustration 3-4. He looked it over and I explained the columns matched up with the titles on the first page. "I think the Decreasing Premium is the best buy," he said. "You've made your point. Let me show it to our company attorney. I can afford the larger early premium to pay less later and get back the gain you showed me."

I asked when I should call back. He said to call him in three or four days. He bought the permanent insurance. But the case does not have a happy ending for me. On advice from advisors in the corporation, whom I tried to meet but couldn't, Len bought from the previous agent who they called back in. Of course, I was disappointed in not getting the case but it proved to me once again that "labeling" on premium basis takes the emphasis off the word "term" and the preconceived thoughts about it.

Illustration 3-3

			$250,000
Increasing Premium (Worst Conversion Options)	Increasing Premium (Best Conversion Options)	Decreasing Premium	Decreasing Premium-Decreasing Insurance $250,000 to $100,000

Total Premiums to Age 65	$77,795	$94,090	$ 72,641	$51,295
Equity	0	0	126,023	50,409

Illustration 3-4

$250,000

	Cheapest Term	Term	OL	$100,000 Ordinary Life With $150,000 Decreasing Term	
1	417.50	720	3653	2202	250062
2	435.00	745	3498	2140	248896
3	502.50	770	3413	2106	247580
4	530.00	790	3328	2072	246115
5	765.00	838	3240	2037	244651
6	820.00	905	3150	2001	242870
7	887.50	995	3103	1982	241089
8	962.50	1095	3055	1963	239014
9	1,042.50	1193	2993	1938	236939
10	1,130.00	1295	2930	1913	234566
11	1,222.50	1400	2863	1886	232042
12	1,327.50	1523	2798	1860	229219
13	1,442.50	1655	2730	1833	226257
14	1,570.00	1785	2635	1795	222995
15	1,712.50	1935	2540	1757	219582

16	1,870.00	2115	2448	1720	215720
17	2,045.00	2338	2353	1682	211707
18	2,235.00	2600	2260	1645	207246
19	2,440.00	2878	2163	1606	202335
20	2,665.00	3198	2065	1567	197124
21	2,910.00	3548	1968	1528	191461
22	3,175.00	3930	1875	1491	195350
23	3,467.50	4370	1778	1452	178799
24	3,787.50	4808	1655	1403	171497
25	4,142.50	5323	1535	1355	193744
26	4,525.00	5960	1418	1308	155240
27	4,947.50	6008	1303	1262	146133
28	5,407.50	6615	1195	1219	136294
29	5,907.50	7145	1043	1158	125553
30	6,452.50	7588	895	1099	113908
31	7,050.00	8023	758	315	101211
Total Premiums to Age 65	77,795.00	94,090	72,641	51,295	
Equity	0.00	0	126,023	50,409	

4

The Land Contract

We will talk about the simple, the complex, and the complicated. The simple, most of us try to do all the time. The complex, I think, is not the worst thing in the world. Some things we present are complex but, if we present them clearly, they will be understood. The complicated creeps into some of the areas that we show and we've got to uncomplicate them. Therefore, when we do complicate them, the selling is rough.

Let's talk about definitions; about how to make things simple. Let's consider a relatively common item, a car. I'm old enough to remember the days when the turn signal was an option. You paid extra for it. If you saw a car coming down the block with a turn signal, you followed that car and you ran after it until it went around the corner. You wanted to see this light blink on and off. That's a fact. There are many things we take for granted today: we have automatic dimming lights that go on and off with the dark, power steering, power brakes.

The automatic transmissions; we didn't have automatic transmissions years ago. I remember once at a funeral when it was time to go to the cemetery there were extra people who needed a ride. One member of the family was riding in one of the limosines and was asked by someone else if they could use his car and drive it to the cemetery. This would have helped those people without a ride. He said, "No, it's got a special transmission." The special transmission was an automatic transmission and because previously you didn't have that—you had to shift gears with a clutch—he thought you would ruin his. All you had to do was shift gears and drive.

Things have changed. Life has become a lot more simple. But at the same time, more complex and more complicated. I've got a car that has a heated mirror on the outside. Years ago to relax, you took a ride. You took your family somewhere. You'd get into the car and drive for an hour. I dare you to do that now. Nobody goes for a ride to relax. You go down any country road or expressway exactly at the speed limit. Be legal and see what happens. Behind you they'll be blowing their horns, and passing you and swearing at you and blinking lights. Today you can't relax taking a ride. Today expressways lead to the bars and psychiatrist's office.

I also remember the days, if you wanted to relax a little bit and do something simple, you would go out to an airport and park in a parking lot and watch the planes come in and out. That was a big evening out before television. I dare you today to take your car and park anywhere for ten minutes and see if you survive. You'll be mugged. Nobody stops their car for ten minutes these days.

So, I've developed a talk to simplify the complex and the complicated and talk about the ordinary life contract and the land contract and the mortgage, if you will, and the term insurance policy as an apartment rental agreement. I did this when I had an interview in 1977 with three large shareholders who operated a real estate firm. One was a lawyer, one was an accountant and one was the actual builder. I wanted to talk in a language they could understand. I think an awful lot of things we take for granted is language the clients don't understand. Such as, "cash value." Many people just don't understand it, no matter how they agree with us or how we talk about it. So we have to put it in their language so they *can* understand it. I did much thinking about this and I try to do this with every interview. I remember one time selling insurance to an Italian restaurant owner and getting nowhere until finally I said, "What's the best pizza you have, how much does it cost?" I forget what the figure was, it was so far back. Let's say five dollars. So he says, "Five dollars."

And I asked, "Do you ever make one of those for somebody on a telephone order, and they are supposed to pick it up later and you get stuck for it?"

He said, "Yah, I get stuck once in awhile."

I said, "Well, all I'm talking about is two pizzas a week that you don't have to cook, you don't even get stuck. And I'm going to give you back a lot of pizzas when you or your family really need them."

And he said, "OK, that's only two pizzas a week."

Ten dollars a week he didn't understand. So you have got to relate things back to terms that the other people understand. And that is what I attempted to do here, as I try to do all the time, by simplifying proceedures and presentations.

The Land Contract

So, let's go. I will switch back and forth from the role of lecturer and teacher to the role of insurance man during an interview. It's going to be interchangeable so just imagine an interview going on. I have three owners in my office and I work off an overhead projector.

"Gentlemen," I say, "I'm going to show you a couple of contracts and I'm going to ask your opinion on them; you know more about them than I do. The first item I'll show you is the actual land contract for my home." (See Illustration 4-1.) They understand this very well because they know how to read these columns. "Now, this is my home. When I moved back to Detroit in 1970, it cost $47,000. I made a $12,000 down payment so I have a $35,000 principal account as of July 1, 1970. The "Starting Balance" is $35,000. Interest is at 7% per annum, pretty good, in those days, by the way. In 1970 it was much like it is today. Interest rates were up to 10%. The seller happened to be a man, age 53, who was retiring and the only thing in the world he wanted was income. So, we worked out a monthly payment of $250.00 to include interest and principal. That's the same land contract I have existing on my house today. He came out with a pretty good deal. It takes 26 years to pay back $35,000 at 7% interest, which will be before July 1, 1995. Look at this column. It takes me $40,227.94 of interest to pay off $35,000. I'm really paying $75,000 for $35,000. They call it 'interest.' It's a good contract at 7%. Simple, easy to understand, first year $2,450.00 in interest, $550.00 on principal and these change as you go along.

"Now, let's talk about contracts of insurance. I call it the Land Contract. (See Illustration 4-2.) It reads, 'This contract dated February, 1976, between Irwin B. Meisel, CLU as agent for Connecticut Mutual Life Insurance Company, whose address is 140 Garden Street, Hartford, Connecticut, and Art A., Jim B. and Tom C. as 33-1/3 percent

Illustration 4-1

	Starting Balance	Interest	Principal	Year-end Balance	
7/1/70	35,000.00	2,450.00	550.00	34,450.00	7/1/71
7/1/71	34,450.00	2,411.50	588.50	33,861.50	7/1/72
7/1/72	33,861.50	2,370.31	629.69	33,231.81	7/1/73
7/1/73	33,231.81	2,326.23	673.77	32,558.04	7/1/74
7/1/74	32,558.04	2,279.06	720.94	31,837.10	7/1/75
7/1/75	31,837.10	2,228.60	771.40	31,065.70	7/1/76
7/1/76	31,065.70	2,174.60	825.40	30,240.30	7/1/77
7/1/77	30,240.30	2,116.82	883.18	29,357.12	7/1/78
7/1/78	29,357.12	2,054.99	945.01	28,412.11	7/1/79
7/1/79	28,412.11	1,988.85	1,011.15	27,400.96	7/1/80
7/1/80	27,400.96	1,918.07	1,081.93	26,319.03	7/1/81
7/1/81	26,319.03	1,842.33	1,157.67	25,161.36	7/1/82
7/1/82	25,161.36	1,761.30	1,238.70	23,922.66	7/1/83
7/1/83	23,922.66	1,674.59	1,325.41	22,597.25	7/1/84
7/1/84	22,597.25	1,581.81	1,418.19	21,179.06	7/1/85
7/1/85	21,179.06	1,482.53	1,517.47	19,661.59	7/1/86
7/1/86	19,661.59	1,376.31	1,623.69	18,037.90	7/1/87

7/1/87	18,037.90	1,262.65	1,737.35	16,300.55	7/1/88
7/1/88	16,300.55	1,141.04	1,858.96	14,441.59	7/1/89
7/1/89	14,441.59	1,010.91	1,989.09	12,452.50	7/1/90
7/1/90	12,452.50	871.68	2,128.32	10,324.18	7/1/91
7/1/91	10,324.18	722.69	2,277.31	8,046.87	7/1/92
7/1/92	8,046.87	563.25	2,436.75	5,610.12	7/1/93
7/1/93	5,610.12	392.71	2,607.29	3,002.83	7/1/94
7/1/94	3,002.83	210.20	2,789.80	213.03	7/1/95
7/1/95	213.03	14.91	213.03	--	
Totals		$40,227.94	$35,000.00		

1. $35,000 principal as of July 1, 1970.

2. Interest at 7% per annum.

3. Monthly payments of $250.00 to include interest and principal.

Illustration 4-2

Land Contract

WITH ALTERNATE TAX AND INSURANCE PROVISIONS

FORM MB-17 REV. 10-15-75

Parties

This Contract, Made this First day of February, 19 76, between Irwin B. Meisel, CLU, as agent for the Connecticut Mutual Life Insurance Company hereinafter referred to as the "Seller," whose address is 140 Garden Street, Hartford, Connecticut and Art A., Jim B., and Tom C., as 33 1/3% shareholders for Comares Corporation hereinafter referred to as the "Purchaser," whose address is 24711 Southeastern Highway, Southfield, Michigan 48017

Witnesseth:

Description of Premises

1. ***THE SELLER AGREES AS FOLLOWS:***

(a) To sell and convey to the Purchaser land in the City ~~Village—Township—~~ of Southfield, Oakland **County, Michigan, described as:** promise to deliver $100,000 immediately at death of named shareholder. Corporation may apply to best use as determined by itself. Intended use is to indemnify corporation against all claims, obligations, and liens by survivors of named shareholder.

together with all tenements, hereditaments, improvements and appurtenances, including all lighting fixtures, plumbing fixtures, shades, Venetian blinds, curtain rods, storm windows, storm doors, screens, awnings, if any, and full services and knowledge of agent, now on the premises, and subject to all applicable building and use restrictions, and easements, if any, affecting the premises.

Terms of Payment

(*b*) That the consideration for the sale of the above described premises to the Purchaser is:

None ($) DOLLARS,

of which the sum of None ($) DOLLARS,

has heretofore been paid to the Seller, the receipt of which is hereby acknowledged, and the balance of

Forty thousand, five hundred four ($40,504) DOLLARS,

is to be paid to the Seller, ~~with~~ as interest ~~on any~~ only part thereof at any time unpaid at the rate of .02665 (2.665%) per cent. per annum while the Purchaser is not in default, and at the rate of .02665 (2.665%) per cent. per annum when and as often as the Purchaser is in default. This ~~balance of purchase money and~~ interest shall be paid in monthly installments of

annual Two thousand, six hundred sixty-five ($2,665.00) DOLLARS

each, or ~~more~~ less at Purchaser's option, on the mutually agreed upon day of each month, beginning February 1, 1976; said payments to be applied first ~~upon~~ only interest and the ~~balance on principal;~~ waived PROVIDED, ~~the entire purchase money~~ and interest shall be fully paid within years from the date hereof, anything herein to the contrary notwithstanding.

Seller's Duty to Convey

(c) Upon receiving payment in full of all sums owing herein, less the amount then due on any existing mortgage or mortgages, and the surrender of the duplicate of this contract, to execute and deliver to the Purchaser or the Purchaser's assigns, a good and sufficient Warranty Deed conveying title to said land, subject to aforesaid restrictions and easements and subject to any then existing mortgage or mortgages, and free from all other encumbrances, except such as may be herein set forth, and except such encumbrances as shall have accrued or attached since the date hereof through the acts or omissions of persons other than the Seller or his assigns.

To furnis[illegible] Title Evid[illegible]

([illegible]d) To d[illegible]liver to the [illegible]urchaser as evidence of title, at th[illegible] Seller's o[illegible], either a Po[illegible] of ~~Title~~ Life [illegible]nsurance or Ab[illegible]t of T[illegible] the effe[illegible] date of [illegible] policy or ce[illegible]ation [illegible] of Abst[illegible] be approxi[illegible] the [illegible] this con[illegible] [illegible]d is[illegible] the ... AB[illegible] AND T[illegible] [illegible]PAN[illegible] [illegible]roit[illegible] shall [illegible] righ[illegible] posse[illegible] shareholders for Comares Corporation.' '' One was 36, one was 40, one was 42. I used the average age of 40.

I wasn't going to get fancy. ''The seller,'' me, agrees as follows: '' 'to sell and convey to the Purchaser property in the township of Southfield, city of Southfield, County of Oakland, Michigan, promise to deliver $100,000 immediately at the death of the named shareholder. Corporation may apply to the best use as determined by itself. Intended use is to indemnify corporation against all claims, obligations and liens by survivors of named shareholder, together with all tenements, hereditaments, improvements, appurtenances, and full services and knowledge of agent. That the consideration for the sale of the above,' this means downpayment which you don't have to make, 'for which the sum of zero is received.' ''

They don't have to give me anything right now. In fact, they owe me $40,504 to be paid out on a schedule. I've doctored this, I have changed that.

''First as interest, 'Paid at the rate of .02665 percent while the purchaser is not in default. Annually, it's $2,665, each or less.' That's the most it can be, '$2,665 or less at purchasers option, on the mutually agreed upon date beginning first of February 1976. First upon interest and the balance on principal is waived.' Anything that you waive, by the way, in a standard contract, is to the benefit of the buyer. Right? Anything you add in may be to his detriment.''

''Seller's duty to convey''; we go through a bunch of language to convey the obligation to furnish title insurance. I changed that. Give us a policy of life insurance. '' 'That the purchaser agrees as follows: To purchase said land' and so forth. I don't think you fellows want to read all of this. It is a standard land contract in which I waived certain things. I have here, I waived, I waived, I waived.'' (This part of the Land Contract is not shown.) ''Everything that you waive in a contract comes out for the benefit of the buyer.

''Let's go to the second page of the Land Contract. (See Illustration 4-3.) Here we have a bunch of other clauses, very legal language. It's the standard thing which I bought at the office supply store. If you want to read all of it, we could, but it has to do with land contracts and mortgages. 'Seller does not have this right'—it doesn't mean anything, I could have just said I waive it. But then, I wanted to doctor the contract. I want to show that ''I'' the seller, do not have this right. 'Assignment by Purchaser' I changed to 'Assignment by Seller. No assignment or conveyance by the seller shall create an incumbrance.' I can't do any assignment; he can but I'll get to that later on.

"Over here another paragraph reads, 'see additional conditions.' Now, since I struck out some things, I have got to put some things in. 'See attached list of additional conditions.' (See Illustrations 4-4, 4-5.) On this attached list of additional conditions it says:

'1) No principal payments,

'2) Decreasing interest payments only.' It started at .02665 or less,

'3) Because of waiver of principal payments and the decreasing payments, the fair market value is going to stay at $100,000, payable immediately at death.' There is going to be no appreciation of the asset because we are lowering the cost each year.

'4) The seller, (me), will buy the asset back at equity value any time on demand notice.' You don't have to look for anybody else, you don't have to look for real estate people or other buyers. I will buy it back, I promise.

'5) The seller, (me), will pay all acquisition and maintenance costs.' All you pay is what is on the front page, .02665 per $100,000 lot.

'6) Purchaser may pay annually, semi-annually, quarterly, or monthly.

'7) The seller will waive these interest payments if the shareholder is disabled. There is an extra cost of $76 a year at the owners option—not required.' "

It is about this time, by the way, the builder in the crowd says, "Well, I won't buy anything without that option. That's tremendous. Are you sure?"

And I said, "Yes."

And he asked, "How do you do that?"

And I replied, "I don't know. It's in your contract."

So he says, "OK." And by the way, I think it is the simplest way of answering objections. It just exists.

" '8) The seller will pay double the fair market value if the shareholder dies accidently. There is an extra cost of $93 a year at the owners option,' your option. It's not required! I want to show how flexible this is. You have the options. The seller has very few options.

'9) The purchaser has the right to stop his interest payments when he chooses and opt for a Stop Loss Fair Market Value instead of equity.' Does everybody know what that is? Paid-up insurance.

'10) Shareholder must pass a medical exam.' Obviously, if we are

Illustration 4-3

Maintenance of Premises

(*g*) To keep and maintain the premises and the buildings thereon in as good condition as they are at the date hereof and not to commit waste, remove or demolish any improvements thereon, or otherwise diminish the value of the Seller's security, without the written consent of the Seller.

3. ***THE SELLER AND PURCHASER MUTUALLY AGREE AS FOLLOWS:***

Mortgage by Seller

(*a*) That the Seller may, at any time during the continuance of this contract encumber said land by mortgage or mortgages to secure not more than the unpaid balance of this contract at the time such mortgage or mortgages are executed. Such mortgage or mortgages shall be payable in not less than three (3) years from date of execution thereof and shall provide for payment of principal and interest in monthly installments which do not exceed such installments provided for in this contract; or on such other terms as may be agreed upon by the Seller and Purchaser, and shall be a first lien upon the land superior to the rights of the Purchaser herein; provided notice of the execution of said mortgage or mortgages containing the name and address of the mortgagee or his agent, the amount of such mortgage or mortgages, the rate of interest and maturity of the principal and interest shall be sent to the Purchaser by registered mail promptly after execution thereof. Purchaser will, on demand, execute any instruments demanded by the Seller, necessary or requisite to subordinate the rights of the Purchaser hereunder to the lien of any such mortgage or mortgages. In event said Purchaser shall refuse to execute any instruments demanded by said Seller and shall refuse to accept such registered mail hereinbefore provided, or said registered mail shall be returned unclaimed, then the Seller may post such notice in two conspicuous places on said premises, and upon making affidavit duly sworn to of such posting, this proceeding shall operate the same as if said Purchaser had consented to the execution of said mortgage or mortgages, and Purchaser's rights shall be subordinate to said mortgage or mortgages as hereinbefore provided. The consent obtained, or subordination as otherwise herein provided, under or by virtue of the foregoing power, shall extend to any and all renewals or extensions or amendments of said mortgage or mortgages, after Seller has given notice to the Purchaser as above provided for giving notice of the execution of said mortgage or mortgages.

Encumbrances on Seller's Title

Seller does not have this right

(*b*) That if the Seller's interest be that of land contract, or now or hereafter be encumbered by mortgage, the Seller shall meet the payments of principal and interest thereon as they mature and produce evidence thereof to the Purchaser on demand, and in default of the Seller said Purchaser may pay the same. Such payments by Purchaser shall be credited on the sums matured or first maturing hereon, with interest at seven per cent. per annum on payments so made. If proceedings are commenced to recover possession or to enforce the payment of such contract or mortgage because of the Seller's default, the Purchaser may at any time thereafter, while such proceedings are pending, encumber said land by mortgage, securing such sum as can be obtained, upon such terms as may be required, and with the proceeds pay and discharge such mortgage, or purchase money lien. Any mortgage so given shall be a first lien upon the land superior to the rights of the Seller therein, and thereafter the Purchaser shall pay the principal and interest on such mortgage so given as they mature, which payments shall be credited on the sums matured or first maturing hereon. When the sum owing hereon is reduced to the amount owing upon such contract or mortgage or owing on any mortgage executed under either of the powers in this contract contained, a conveyance shall be made in the form above provided containing a covenant by the grantee to assume and agree to pay the same.

Seller   Article 14 of additional condts.

Assignment by ~~Purchaser~~ Seller

(*d*) No assignment or conveyance by the ~~Purchaser~~ Seller shall create any liability whatsoever against the Seller until a duplicate thereof, duly witnessed and acknowledged, together with the residence address of such assignee, shall be delivered to the Seller. Purchaser's liability hereunder shall not be released or affected in any way by delivery of such assignment, or by Seller's endorsement of receipt and/or acceptance thereon.

Possession Waived

(*e*) The Purchaser shall have the right to possession of the premises from and after the date hereof, unless otherwise herein provided, and be entitled to retain possession thereof only so long as there is no default on his part in carrying out the terms and conditions hereof. In the event the premises hereinabove described are vacant or unimproved, the Purchaser shall be deemed to be in constructive possession only, which possessory right shall cease and terminate after service of a notice of forfeiture of this contract. Erection of signs by Purchaser on vacant or unimproved property shall not constitute actual possession by him.

Right to Forfeit Waived See additional Conditions

(*f*) If the Purchaser shall fail to perform this contract or any part thereof, the Seller immediately after such default shall have the right to declare the same forfeited and void, and retain whatever may have been paid hereon, and all improvements that may have been made upon the premises, together with additions and accretions thereto, and consider and treat the Purchaser as his tenant holding over without permission and may take immediate possession of the premises, and the Purchaser and each and every other occupant removed and put out. In all cases where a notice of forfeiture is relied upon by the Seller to terminate rights hereunder, such notice shall specify all unpaid moneys and other breaches of this contract and shall declare forfeiture of this contract effective in fifteen days after service unless such money is paid and any other breaches of this contract are cured within that time.

Acceleration Clause Forbidden

(*g*) ~~If default is made by the Purchaser and such default continues for a period of forty-five days or more, and the Seller desires to foreclose this contract in equity, then the Seller shall have at his option the right to declare the entire unpaid balance hereunder to be due and payable forthwith, notwithstanding anything herein contained to the contrary~~

(*h*) ~~The wife of the Seller, for a valuable consideration, joins herein and agrees to join in the execution of the deed to be made in fulfillment hereof~~.

(*i*) Time shall be deemed to be of the essence of this contract.

(*j*) ~~The individual parties hereto represent themselves to be of full age, and the corporate parties hereto represent themselves to be valid existing corporations with their charters in full force and effect~~.

Notice to Purchaser

(*k*) Any declarations, notices or papers necessary or proper to terminate, accelerate or enforce this contract shall be presumed conclusively to have been served upon the Purchaser if such instrument is enclosed in an envelope with first class postage fully prepaid, if said envelope is addressed to the Purchaser at the address set forth in the heading of this contract or at the latest other address which may have been specified by the Purchaser and receipted for in writing by the Seller, and said envelope is deposited in a United States Post Office Box.

Add[…] Se[…]tac[…] lis[…]f addi[…]onal […]ondi[…]

going to do all these things, waive things, charge interest only, buy it back from you, guarantee $100,000 and you are only paying $2600 per year; if someone should die, we want a medical exam. We want to give these lots to people we think we can get our money out of. All we ask is $40,000 altogether. You have got to pass a medical exam.

'11) Purchaser (you) may demand that the seller (me) rent the property from purchaser at age 65 by leaving the equity in the contract. The shareholder will receive $325.65 a month rent or $3,907.80 yearly for life.' "We spell out the yearly because you are paying yearly premiums on the front, $2665. I want to show that the client gets more back in any event." 'Ten years payment minimum, guaranteed to shareholder's survivor if he dies prior to age 75.

'12) Seller may not sell, change, or revoke the contract to any third party.

'13) Purchaser may sell, change, revoke, assign, pledge, cancel at any time.

'14) Purchaser may borrow back the interest payments to extent of 92% of equity account; on demand.' That's pretty good. Make a payment and borrow it back.

'15) After the second year, the purchaser may skip payment of interest, in case of hardship. Cost of 8% deductible of the interest skipped.' You skip a payment and deduct the interest.

'16) The purchaser has the right to renew the contract after age 65, the interest continues to decrease, the equity continues to increase, the fair market value remains the same.

'17) All purchaser's payments cease at death.' If the contract holder should die at anytime the contract is in force, all of his payments stop and $100,000 is paid immediately to his named successor. This is true at anytime; even if only one monthly payment has been made in the first year of the contract.

"Now, here is the schedule and the numbers. (See Illustration 4-4.) In 1976 the contract says you owe me $40,504. It will be paid off in the year 2001. You will have paid all these payments and it has gone to $40,504 interest payments or "Balance of Contract." The first year you pay me $2665. You will have an equity column of $1,040. Give me $2,665, I give you $1,040. Equity in your house, in your contract. Stop Loss Fair Market Value: if you say, 'I want to quit' the first year, buy a piece of the action, you have $2,537 worth or 2.5%. The estate value is $100,000.

"The second year you only owe me $39,848. Interest payments have come down to $2,497. Equity is up to $3,321. Your Stop Loss Fair Market Value is up to $7,869, and the estate value is $100,000, as it is throughout.

"Go down a few years. Let's say to 1988. You still owe me $27,444. But, if you die in that year you don't owe me anything else. The family or the corporation has $100,000. The interest payment has come down to $1,620 at a time when inflation has probably taken things up. You have equity of $27,041. If you want to quit, I'll buy it back, immediately, I said so in the contract. The Stop Loss Fair Market Value is $47,185. The estate value is still $100,000.

"By the year 2001 you will have owed me $40,504 and will have paid me $40,504. You paid what you bargained for. And from day one you owned a $100,000 piece of property. If you died, everything else stopped. You owed $40,504 and you paid $40,504 and you got an equity of $54,919. Compare that with a $35,000 land contract for which I paid $75,000 and had an equity of $35,000. I guarantee it today. If you want to stop at age 65, your piece of the action is worth $74,196. If you don't want to sell the equity back to me, you have a $74,196 piece of property with a clear title."

The builder in the crowd said, " Well, wait a minute. Look over here. In this third year, we are going to pay in $2,422 and it is going to go up from $3,300 to $5,600."

I said, "Yes."

The builder said, "That's $2,300."

I said "Yes."

"How can you do that?"

I responded, "I don't know."

The builder asked, "It seems amazing. How does it work?"

I said, "I don't know, it just does."

"Let's look over at 1983 when it is about $2,000. You paid $2,028 this year and it has gone up from $13,740 to $15,864. You are getting back now what you have put in. But, this isn't the end of this contract. It might be too expensive for you. You might decide to rent. And if you decide to rent, you have got to have an apartment lease. You cannot move into an apartment without a lease. Can you?

Illustration 4-4

Use this Acknowledgment Form for Individuals

STATE OF MICHIGAN

COUNTY OF ________________ } ss.

On this ________ day of ________ in the year One Thousand Nine Hundred ________

before me, the subscriber, a Notary Public in and for said County, appeared ________

____

____

to ... wn ... e per... escrib... and wh... ed th... going ... and ... ely ... ged th

PAYMENT SCHEDULE

PAYABLE AT ________________

Unless notified by Seller in writing to the contrary.

DATE	PRINCIPAL PAYMENTS	BALANCE OF PRINCIPAL Contract	INTEREST PAYMENTS Rate 2.665%	PAYING INTEREST TO Equity	Stop Loss Fair Mkt. Value (SIGNATURE)	Estate Value
1976	-0-	40,504	2,665	1,040	2,537	100,000
1977	-0-	39,848	2,497	3,321	7,869	100,000
1978	-0-	39,150	2,422	5,642	12,989	100,000
1979	-0-	38,406	2,345	7,605	17,014	100,000
1980	-0-	37,612	2,267	9,609	20,894	100,000

1981	-0-	36,522	2,189	11,654	24,634	100,000
1982	-0-	35,396	2,110	13,740	28,240	100,000
1983	-0-	34,238	2,028	15,864	31,709	100,000
1984	-0-	33,027	1,946	18,027	35,051	100,000
1985	-0-	31,762	1,865	20,226	38,264	100,000
1986	-0-	30,412	1,785	22,462	41,355	100,000
1987	-0-	28,973	1,705	24,734	44,328	100,000
1988	-0-	27,444	1,620	27,041	47,185	100,000
1989	-0-	25,824	1,529	29,384	49,933	100,000
1990	-0-	24,119	1,439	31,764	52,577	100,000
1991	-0-	22,334	1,350	34,180	55,118	100,000
1992	-0-	20,469	1,265	36,632	57,560	100,000
1993	-0-	18,523	1,211	39,121	59,907	100,000
1994	-0-	16,495	1,158	41,646	62,160	100,000
1995	-0-	14,385	1,126	44,211	64,326	100,000
1996	-0-	12,196	1,090	46,364	66,416	100,000
1997	-0-	9,929	794	48,512	68,444	100,000
1998	-0-	7,584	744	50,654	70,414	100,000
1999	-0-	5,162	698	52,790	72,330	100,000
2000	-0-	2,665	656	54,919	74,196	100,000
2001	-0-	-0-	-0-	54,919	74,196	100,000
Totals		40,504	40,504	54,919	74,196	

Illustration 4-5

Additional Conditions of Contract:

1. No principal payments.
2. Decreasing interest payments only.
3. Because of waiver of principal payments and decreasing interest payments, fair market value stays at $100,000 payable immediately at death.
4. Seller will buy asset back at equity value any time on demand notice.
5. Seller will pay all acquisition and maintenance costs.
6. Purchaser may pay annually, semi-annually, quarterly or monthly.
7. Seller will waive interest payments if shareholder is disabled - extra cost $76/year (Owners option - not required).
8. Seller will pay double fair market value if shareholder dies accidentally - extra cost $93/year (Owners option - not required).
9. Purchaser has right to stop interest payments and opt for "Stop Loss Fair Market Value" instead of equity.
10. Shareholder must pass a medical exam.

11. Purchaser may demand that seller rent property from purchaser at age 65 by leaving equity in contract. Shareholder will receive $325.65 monthly rent ($3,907.80 yearly) for life. Ten (10) years payment minimum, guaranteed to shareholder's survivor if he dies prior to age 75.

12. Seller may not sell, change, or revoke contract to any third party.

13. Purchaser may sell, change, revoke, assign, pledge, cancel at any time.

14. Purchaser may borrow back interest payments to extent of 92% of equity account; on demand.

15. After second year, purchaser may skip payment of interest, in case of hardship. Cost of 8% (deductible) of interest skipped.

16. Purchaser has the right to renew the contract after age 65, interest continues to decrease, equity continues to increase, fair market value remains the same.

17. All purchaser's payments cease at death of purchaser.

The Apartment Lease

"'So here's the apartment lease. It reads, in part: (See Illustration 4-6.) 'Made between the Connecticut Mutual Life Insurance Company and the name of the shareholder. The following apartment of $100,000 in a building located in Southfield, Michigan, 48077. For a term beginning the 1st of February, 1976, and ending the 31st of January, 2006, provided that you could use the property as outlined. In case rent shall be due and unpaid, default of 31 days is considered late payment. To pay the Landlord as rental for said premises, the sum of $371 per year, upon delivery and an increasing sum on the first day of each calendar year thereafter.' The increasing schedule is attached which I'll show you. 'To use and occupy the said premises by not more than, *unlimited.'* You can get as many of these apartments as you want. 'That the tenant may assign and sublet any or all part of it, whatever he chooses.' You have that right. You have a right to examine the property. 'Tenant agrees not to violate any of the ordinances of the municipality where the property is located in the State of Michigan as well as the United States;' you have to agree to that. 'Tenant disagrees that the Landlord or any of his agents have the right to enter said premises and inspect and look it over.

"'That any alterations or additional locks or bolts or so forth; you can make all the alterations you want, up to $100,000 worth. Tenant disagrees that in the event to cut off and stop heat and so forth; you don't have to read it because I said you will disagree to it. There are a lot of other conditions which I struck out. Anything you strike out is good for the tenant. Anything you put in is good for the landlord. They have a few more conditions here. (Entire Apartment Lease is not reproduced.) As you can see, I struck them out. I don't want to make this contract too tough. Landlord acknowledges receipt of no dollars so far, which means no security deposit. By the way, the tenant shall hold this property after the expiration of the terms demised and so forth, for a period of thirty years and no longer. I'll only give you a thirty year lease. The rest of it is legal language which doesn't make any difference.

"'Now we will get down to the actual conditions of things I have added in order to make this feasible for only $371 a year. (See Illustration 4-7.)

'1) No principal payments.' You don't have to pay me any principal. Just this interest or rent or whatever you want to call it but, you don't get involved in my cost of this building.

'2) There is an increasing rental payment. $371 is for the first year and it goes up. We'll call it the annual cost of living adjustment.

'3) The Fair Market Value stays at $100,000 which is payable (given over) at death to family of lessee.

'4) The lessor (we) will pay all acquisition and maintenance costs.

'5) The lessee (you) may pay rent annually, semi-annually, quarterly or monthly.

'6) The lessor will provide rent free premises if the lessee becomes disabled, an extra cost of $49 per year accelerating, optional.' You don't have to have it.

'7) Lessor will give over fair market value of two apartments if lessee dies accidentally, at an extra cost of $80 per year—optional.' You don't have to have it.

'8) The lessee shall have no portion of rent applied to equity or stop loss provision.' I'll show you that in a schedule I have.

'9) The lessee must pass a medical exam. Here for sure. We are renting to you, for $371, $100,000 worth of property and if you die your family has it. We have to make sure that you are in good health." (The remaining six conditions may be examined on Illustration 4-7.)

"Those are the conditions that we put in and now for the schedule. (See Illustration 4-8.) It's got to cost some money yet it's cheap. In 1977, your Annual Rent is $371 with nothing applied to Principal and nothing applied to Stop Loss Fair Market Value. You have an Estate Value of $100,000. But $371 is cheap. It goes up the next year to $401, which isn't that bad. $432, $466, that isn't bad. In the year 2007 we have got to evict you. You still have no Principal, no Equity, no Stop Loss Fair Market Value and a $100,000 Estate Value. You made rent payments to us of $52,751. I assumed during that time, since you rented or leased, you had been investing the difference, somewhere. So, you are going to have some principal and equity elsewhere. The builder in the crowd said, "It doesn't seem too good to me. $52,000 to get nothing back."

I have these papers in blue, legal binders. He took his and he put it aside and said, "Let's not look at that one. We are not too concerned about that—we build things. We don't rent anything; we own. Let's look at that other schedule again."

I immediately knew I didn't have a term sale. If you noticed, I moved directly from the ordinary Land Contract to the term (Apartment Rental) without any question about what to do. I just explained both sides. So far, I haven't had any term sales from using this idea.

Illustration 4-6

APARTMENT LEASE

THIS LEASE, WITNESSETH: That Connecticut Mutual Life Insurance Company

hereinafter designated as the Landlord does hereby let and lease to Art A., Jim B., and Tom C.

For Comares Corporation, hereinafter designated as the Tenant, the

following apartment $100,000 in a building located at 24711 Southeastern Highway

Southfield, ________, Michigan, 48077

for a term beginning the 1st day of February, 1976,

and ending the 31st day of January, ~~19~~ 2006

to be used and occupied for residential purposes only.

PROVIDED, in case any rent shall be due and unpaid or default be made in any of the covenants herein contained, then it shall be lawful for the Landlord, his certain attorney, legal representatives and assigns, to re-enter into, possess the said premises and the Tenant and each and every occupant to remove and put out. (31 days is considered late payment.)

The Tenant hereby hires said premises for the term aforesaid, and covenants:

1. To pay the Landlord as rental for said premises the sum of $371.00 yr. (Three hundred and seventy one) Dollars upon delivery hereof, and ~~a like sum~~ an increasing sum in advance on the first day of each calendar month thereafter during the term thereof to be paid the Landlord or his authorized agent. (Increasing schedule attached.)

2. To use and occupy the said premises by not more than unlimited persons and their future issue and for the purposes for which they are let. Also, to keep the premises in accordance with all police, sanitary and other regulations imposed by any government authority and comply with all reasonable rules and regulations of the Landlord.

3. That the Tenant ~~will not~~ may assign this lease ~~nor~~ and sublet the premises ~~nor~~ or any part thereof without the consent of the Landlord thereto endorsed hereon in writing.

4. That the Tenant has examined the premises as to the condition, and as to the equipment and appurtenances, and acknowledges that they have been received in good condition, except as otherwise specified in writing, and Tenant agrees that during the continuance of this agreement said premises and any and every part thereof will be kept in as good repair at Tenant's expense as when taken, reasonable use and wear thereof and damage by the elements excepted; and that Tenant will not allow any waste, misuse or neglect of anything furnished by the Landlord, and will pay for all damages to the premises or equipment, or damages to any other Tenant or other persons caused by such waste, misuse or neglect.

5. Tenant agrees not to violate any of the ordinances of the municipality where the property is located or of the State of Michigan or United States, nor permit premises to be used for any unlawful or immoral purposes whatsoever, or for any purpose that will injure the reputation of the said premises or the neighborhood.

6. Tenant ~~agrees~~ disagrees that the Landlord or any of his agents shall have the right to enter said premises during all reasonable hour[illegible] examin[illegible] protec[illegible] the same, [illegible] show to prospective bu[illegible]ers or r[illegible]ers, or t[illegible] such repa[illegible] additio[illegible] alterations as [illegible] deem[illegible] [illegible]ess[illegible] [illegible]aid [illegible] or [illegible]nts.

Illustration 4-7

Conditions of Apartment Lease:

1. No principal payments.
2. Increasing rental payments (annual cost of living adjustment).
3. Fair market value stays at $100,000, payable (given over) at death to family of lessee.
4. Lessor will pay all acquisition and maintenance costs.
5. Lessee may pay rent annually, semi-annually, quarterly, or monthly.
6. Lessor will provide rent free premises if lessee becomes disabled - extra cost $49/year accelerating (Optional).
7. Lessor will give over fair market value of two apartments if lessee dies accidentally - extra cost $80/year (Optional).
8. Lessee shall have no portion of rent applied to equity or stop loss provision.
9. Lessee must pass a medical exam.
10. Lessor may not sell, pledge, or assign property.
11. Lessee may revoke, pledge, assign or cancel at any time.

12. Lessor will evict all tentants on their 70th birthday.

13. Lessee may exercise option to buy property prior to age 65. Lessor may charge no more than interest payments for any healthy new mortgagee of same attained age. No medical evidence required.

14. If lessee misses any rent payments, lessor will evict lessee after 31 days of such delinquency. Lessee may request right to re-occupy but must re-establish good health and moral record.

15. All rent payments cease immediately on death of tenant. Entire value of apartment, ($100,000) is paid to tentant's name survivor.

I showed them a $100,000 lot because I didn't know what their business was worth. I wanted that to come out.

We went back to the first schedule and the builder said, "You mean in this first year, if we want fifteen of those lots, (immediately, I knew this business was worth one and one-half million dollars) we've got to pay 15 times that, about $40,000?"

I said, "Yes."

"OK," he answered, "let's go to where you show $2,000 of cost. That year we'll pay $30,000. And it is going to go up $2,000 per lot or about $30,000?"

And I said, "Yes."

He continued. "And in our second year, it goes up $1500? We are putting in $2400?"

I said "Yes."

"And we are putting in 15 times that, say $36,000, to get back $25,000?"

I said "Yes."

The builder thought for a moment then said, "Let me tell you something, guys. Anytime this corporation can't stand to lay out $36,000 to get back $25,000 and have a million and a half dollars worth of property, we're in trouble."

So I said, "OK, it sounds like you are going to go ahead with that. But, before we do, I've got to know what we are talking about. It's a lot of property—a million and a half dollars. And I want you to know who you are talking to. So here you are, here is my application. I want to go to work for you. (As I say the following I show them a copy of my resumé.) There's my name, my telephone number, my address, my social security number, and also, how much I am going to charge you. I get paid for this, I don't do it gratis. I am going to charge you one pecent of the principal amount we are talking about. We actually write it into these things. Here is my background, there is where I went to school, how long I stayed in school, and so forth. Here's my present employer from 1956 to present, including my work for the U.S. Army, where I went to school and some references. If you choose to check on me you can call Mr. John Marshall, he owns One Way Industries. There is his telephone number and his address. Lawrence Traison, Walker Printery; there is his telephone number and address. Nathan Light, there's his company, there is his address; you can call him if you choose. Here's some more information on me. My wife's name and information on her. And so forth.

"So Gentlemen, I want to go to work for one percent. Here is my application, I need yours." And the answer was, "OK." I sold them a million and a half case. That's the Land Contract presentation.

This Land Contract-Apartment Rental presentation has proven to be primarily a one-interview close. It seems to be adaptable to any purpose and seems to answer all questions in a purely logical fashion. I think this idea is original with me. I have taken nothing of it from anyone else. But we must all be honest; I think all of it came from other people who have tried other ideas along similar lines since the whole concept is Permanent or Temporary. I believe, through assimilation, this idea just developed.

Illustration 4-8

Apartment Rental Agreement

$100,000 Apartment

Year	Annual Rent	Principal	Equity	Stop Loss Fair Market Value	Estate Value
1977	371	0	0	0	100,000
1978	401	0	0	0	100,000
1979	432	0	0	0	100,000
1980	466	0	0	0	100,000
1981	503	0	0	0	100,000
1982	544	0	0	0	100,000
1983	594	0	0	0	100,000
1984	640	0	0	0	100,000
1985	692	0	0	0	100,000
1986	751	0	0	0	100,000
1987	819	0	0	0	100,000
1988	898	0	0	0	100,000
1989	980	0	0	0	100,000
1990	1,072	0	0	0	100,000

1991	1,174	0	0	0	100,000
1992	1,288	0	0	0	100,000
1993	1,437	0	0	0	100,000
1994	1,598	0	0	0	100,000
1995	1,775	0	0	0	100,000
1996	1,968	0	0	0	100,000
1997	2,177	0	0	0	100,000
1998	2,455	0	0	0	100,000
1999	2,650	0	0	0	100,000
2000	2,907	0	0	0	100,000
2001	3,200	0	0	0	100,000
2002	3,516	0	0	0	100,000
2003	3,820	0	0	0	100,000
2004	4,142	0	0	0	100,000
2005	4,514	0	0	0	100,000
2006	4,967	0	0	0	100,000
2007	Eviction	---	---	---	-----
Totals	$52,751	0	0	0	0

5

"Yes, but . . .!"

In this chapter I hope to pass on to you some answers to objections that are powerful and have proven to work. Not all agents can use the same answers and all answers are not universal. The same logic will not work for all prospects. If it would we, as salesmen, would have a very simple job; just memorize all the answers to all the objections and spit them out on the proper cue. If they would then work, we would no longer be salesmen but school children who did our homework. After all, when teacher gives a list of fifty spelling words to her students on Monday and then tests these words on Friday, the result is obvious. Those pupils who spent the time memorizing will get them all right. If you had words to memorize and got them all right, you were perfect. You couldn't do any better so you were successful.

Spelling is an exact science; selling isn't. You may be able to spell but you still may not be able to sell. So memorizing every answer to every possible objection will not guarantee a sale on every interview although, we must admit, it will increase the odds in the salesman's favor. A naked answer without emotion, timing, backup logic, and sometimes repetition, is almost useless. Take, for example, the most common objection: "I can't afford it." Take, for example, the most common answer which we, everyone of us learned: "Can you afford to be without it?" When I first learned that answer from my first supervisor, Bill Schonsheck, CLU, I thought the words were golden. I felt I had just discovered the key to selling. All I had to do was get everyone to say to me, "I can't afford it." I quickly learned that not everyone used that objection. I believed the logic, I couldn't afford to be without it, but I must have been saying it wrong because I didn't sell every interview.

As I started to hear more varied and more imaginative objections I started to get my education in the rejection syndrome. I quickly learned that sometimes one answer alone was not enough and sometimes different answers to the same objection were necessary. We then have to add another variable; different types of people. And so the complexity begins. Also, we have to gauge the person's motives when he gives the objection. Sometimes, they're serious. Sometimes, they're stalling. Sometimes, they're testing. Sometimes, they're true. One thing for sure is that we have to find the real objection before any amount of logic or verbiage is going to make any sense.

Some of our answers are merely for the purpose of getting the prospective buyer to talk more until he answers his own question or comes to a serious point in the discussion. A great way of doing this is to ask, "Besides that, is there any other reason?" If there are additional reasons, let them come out. This does one thing; it lets the prospect know you're listening attentively. It also lets him know that you don't want to avoid the issue. I believe this is called communicating.

Another way of handling objections is to carry them to a point farther than the prospect wanted you to. For example, he says, "What if I can't pay a premium a couple of years from now?" I respond, "That's a very valid concern but what if you can't pay any premiums a couple of years from now because of a total disability . . . etc?" Then explain waiver of premium or automatic premium, or guaranteed values. In this fashion you lend validity to his question and it gives you additional points to discuss.

Consider this answer to the large estate owner and see if it takes him farther than his objection. "I can't afford to pay that premium in my tax bracket." Response: "I agree with you that income taxes are terrible but at least we have withholding to take care of the bunching problem. What I'm talking about is estate taxes and the government allows withholding on them, too. Not only withholding but a forgiveness of the tax if you allow the withholding. They call it premium."

Most answers fall into the, "Yes, but . . ." category. That is a tacit agreement and a continuation of the dialogue until another close is reached. The best people in the world at the "Yes, but . . ." methods are kids. Have you ever heard a child who wants to go out at night or wants to have a new stereo? Mother can say, "No" and Junior can say, "Yes, but . . ." and go right on with all the answers and illogical reasons in the world but with a persistance known only to the truly master salespeople of the world. Las Vegas says the odds in this situation are 10 to 1 for the kid. I also put my nickle on the little predator.

We never stop hearing great answers to objections. I copy them all the time from meetings, MDRT tapes, newspapers, TV and observations of life in general. I hear so many I forget them. I try to use as many as I can and in this way keep them fresh. A few years ago I started writing answers to objections and inspirational sayings on 3× 5 flash cards and keeping them in my desk. Saving them is one thing but using them is another, so let me tell you how I force my lazy half to study them.

Every day everyone of us gets put on hold while talking on the telephone. I have a speaker unit on my phone so I can talk without holding it; this is an extremely helpful tool when referring to files or rate books. Now, when I get put on hold, I immediately put the phone on auto pilot and reach for my flash cards. I sometimes get one, two, or three minutes to study. As soon as a voice comes on the line I put the cards away and resume the conversation. If I get on hold a few times a day, I have fifteen or twenty minutes to study. Another thing happens, too. The light on the switchboard is on for my line and my own associates and staff think I'm talking and don't bother me. I've found these few minutes of study each day are valuable since we all promise ourselves we're going to do more studying and reading. We also know that as we study, within a few days or weeks, an opportunity will present itself to use that available knowledge. Is it just coincidence or merely more exposure and awareness?

Just for a moment let me recite how I used wasted time and regimentation to get my CLU designation in two years. In 1972, I started my studies using the self-study method. I had attended one class, gotten the assignment, done the homework, and eagerly attended the next week's class. I was eager and wanted to hear what the instructor had to say to amplify on the material. Unfortunately, not everyone had done their homework. As a result, we did not finish the assigned material, let alone have a good cross discussion. I decided no more class for me. I emphasize, this was my method and I do not recommend it for everyone. I do recommend it, however, for supplemental work. I got my diploma in my car using the following habits.

I found a good partner who wanted to use the same study method as I. Tom Bohs, CLU, and I decided to take two and three classes at a time. Early every Saturday I went to my office to work. At noon I played racquetball. I was home about 3 p.m., at which time I read one assignment. On Sunday morning I read the second subject. Tom and I would meet every Wednesday to review the study guide and test each other. We talked and overtalked all around the material and had a tape recorder going all the time.

For a whole week I would drive around in my car listening to Tom's voice and mine through the car speakers through a tape machine I installed ($75, deductible). When the tape finished, I would start it again. During the course of the week I would hear a jam-packed tape at least four or five times. I utilized the normally wasteful driving time to study and finished studying for my diploma in only two years. I never thought it was tough, although I do admit there was one drawback. I didn't learn the new McDonald's or Coke slogans, but I did get my work done. Everything in life has a price.

I still use my car for the study of Keeping Current tapes, MDRT tapes, CLU tapes, and ones I make myself by reading subjects out loud. I always have company in my car. Some of the greatest insurance and other sales illuminaries are always travelling with me. So, just like the hold button on the telephone, I look forward to my driving time. I recommend the method. If one is serious, it takes a little time and $75, deductible. I follow the old Chinese proverb of "Study as if you could never learn all you wanted to learn and review as if you had forgotten all you have studied."

Let me list some of the flash cards I have in my collection. Most of these are not original with me; only about twenty-five percent are mine.

> I deal primarily in the "success" market.

> You've got too much risk and I'm going to sell the risk to an insurance company.

> The same wife who does not want life insurance at the time the life insurance man proposes it definitely wants it at the time of divorce.

Life insurance and disability insurance is a business decision today and it's an emotional decision tomorrow.

Not buying a plan is self-insurance.

The ultimate in deflation takes place at the time of death of the breadwinner, coincidentally, the ultimate in inflation of a life insurance policy takes place at the same time.

Insurance men bring people to ownership of their own lives by making them aware of things they didn't know they could do before.

If you tried to sell Social Security, they'd put you in jail; but they wouldn't have to because the consumer would not buy it.

I want to challenge you with the idea of owning one million dollars of life insurance.

Do you want to rob your family of the excess value of this corporation because you "can't afford" to buy more life insurance?

It's obvious from the things we discussed that you have some needs and problems, and somewhere in this whole scheme you need $300,000 or $400,000 of security.

In order to get yourself out of a slump, sell something! Probably, insurance—in any amount! Even a $1,000 application can cure a bad mood.

If that doesn't work, buy something! Even a tie may change your mood.

Fresh start is the attitude created.

Discounted dollars—income tax free! Estate tax free!

As you go down the road of life, the theory goes out the window and the practical comes into being.

Section 6166
Buy now, pay later plan. This is the lure. Almost to the point where you think you won't have to pay it. Section 6166 shifts the burdens to the next generation. Bite the bullet and buy the insurance now!

Have your cake and eat it too. (Split-dollar insurance)

Life insurance is passing the hat before death.

Sales Idea—Send out letters to the wives of prominent men offering financial analysis, estate planning for the husbands on a no-charge basis for the lady's benefit.

$200,000 is a lot of money, but it doesn't cost much to buy $200,000.

By buying life insurance your destiny is within your control.

You ask me how much a life insurance policy costs? It's merely the price tag you pay for loving somebody.

No life insurance man earns his commission when he sells the policy, he just *makes* his commission. He *earns* his commission when he gives service on the policy.

You'll be a bigger person than you've ever been.

Prospective widows

Preventive salesmanship or corrective salesmanship.

Term insurance is the most inflexible insurance you can buy. Permanent insurance is the most flexible.

The installment buy-out of purchasing a business interest after the death of a shareholder is booking a new liability at the very moment the corporation can least afford it.

Paying estate taxes is purely voluntary. You can pay the premiums and avoid the taxes.

The only income-producing asset in this business has a heart and it may stop.

That's the old-fashioned idea and approach about life insurance.

Do it the hard way—it's easiest.

Accountants and attorneys look at estate planning as a process of how to transform assets into liquidity. Insurance men look at estate planning as a process of how to create liquidity and keep the assets that one already has.

Excellence is my standard and time is my variable.

Can you describe your insurance program and practices and what you want your insurance to accomplish for your family and yourself?

Being a fair-minded man, assuming insurance were free, how much would you feel would be an adequate amount for your family to have?

Income is your most important asset!

I know that you are too young to die and immune from disability.

Sensitive listening

Problems with lawyers recommending not to buy life insurance? A life insurance policy is a promise to pay. My company will give you a policy which is the promise to pay. Will your lawyer give you the same? What are we really talking about?

Are you looking for an excuse to say no?

Until death do you part

For people who stall:
Make an appointment with yourself. Let's make an appointment right now with yourself when you are going to think it over when no one else is present. Put it on your calendar right now."

Estate planning is tax reform and fiscal reform.

If you don't do something about taking care of your estate the government will come in and have a garage sale. At a garage sale people want the best asset for the best price or the least price.

It's so terribly difficult to run a company with money, but it's virtually impossible to run it without money.

Answer for the accountant who says, "You don't need life insurance":

"You can pay for the value of this stock after death on a ten-year or five-year stretch."

"You now have made a $225,000 problem out of a $100,000 problem."

Using assets other than life insurance to pay estate tax or any other clearance cost only robs the estate of the value of that asset today plus the interest that could be earned from that asset.

A cat has nine lives, but a human being only has one. You better protect it and insure it.

You have borrowed money from the bank. Therefore, you have created a debt structure. However, this structure is in favor of the bank. So, we have to find some way to unstructure and hold on to your business and your estate. We can do this for far less than the interest they are charging.

How much do you own and how much do you owe?

Statement: "My attorney keeps me advised of new things."
Answer: "So does mine. Let's get together and compare notes."

Getting rid of it can be almost as expensive as building it up. It takes time, money and it's expensive.

Each business has three values.

1. The "Going Concern" value,
2. The Liquidation Value,
3. More important than the Liquidation Value, the *Gone value* if they don't make preparations for the successful continuity of the business.

Your estate has a high "paper" value and low "cash" value.

"Either I will find a way . . . or I will make one."

Sir Philip Sydney

What can be done by man can be done by Meisel.

ALL PURPOSE ONE-WORD ANSWER

Sometimes the objection we hear is an absolute stall. The prospect is just objecting or saying something because he thinks he has to say something. It just isn't proper to allow a salesman to be so sincere and convincing that he leaves one nothing to say. Very often these phony, meaningless objections come from friends or relatives or people who are particularly close to you. In effect, they are begging and really say, "You're right, but please let me off the hook."

My one word answer to this objection is, "Baloney." I really use it. But I must caution you that this is one word that must be used with extremely proper timing. In other words, you cannot use it in the wrong place. It will backfire and end all communications. But with the staller and procrastinator that you recognize as such, use it and remain silent after you say it. It will evoke more conversation on his part and usually lead to the true thoughts. One thing for sure is that he won't use any more silly objections for fear that you'll squash him again.

I HAVE A FRIEND IN THE BUSINESS

This is another objection we hear frequently and is a hard one with which to deal. Consider this lengthy answer which has all the elements necessary to keep the prospect's attention and help get the appointment for you.

"Mel, I think it's great that you have a friend in the business. Whether you realize it or not, you have many friends in the business. Who wouldn't want to do business with a successful young man like you. But I have to tell you, this was no random call. I thought carefully about your wife Rhonda and the kids, Arthur and Billy, before I called on you. I like your family and I want to give them the benefit of the best knowledge and service I can. You know, when I do my income tax, I have no objection to what I have to pay if it's the right amount. But I always have the lingering feeling that someone else is getting more deductions than I am just because I don't know all the proper ones. I want to meet with you for sixty minutes (an hour is a big thing but a minute is small) with the provision that either one of us can call off the appointment whenever we want. If I have ideas that will profit your family, you'll naturally want to adopt them. If you've already done them, you'll feel good about your previous wise decisions. Fair enough?"

Moral: More objections mean more appointments, mean more sales, mean more business, mean more referrals.

No objections, no interviews, no sales, no business, no referrals, no way.

6

Games People Play

Shakespeare said, "All the world is a stage . . ." We've all heard the expression about playing on your own home field. Big business says, "The ball is in your court." We refer to people as "winners" or "losers." Life is a competition. Shakespeare could just as easily have said that the whole world was a game and all the people were the players. It's true; we go through the serious business of living by competing with each other, by competing with ourselves, and sometimes tricking ourselves with little ploys and games. Mothers make a game out of which child can cleanup the fastest or pick up the most toys. Sibling rivalry is the most basic and natural kind of game. We can read books such as *The Complete Book of Games*, but the games that go on in the selling arena will never be complete or unimaginative.

This goes both for the salesmen and for the customers. Probably as you're reading this right now, your agency or company is in the midst of a competition, or has just finished one or is just starting one. The toughest manager I ever heard of started his agency meeting announcing the latest contest with the line, "The top three guys get to stay." We set quotas for ourselves. We compete with other agents, sometimes anonomously. But the really funny games are the ones the clients play with us in trying to convince us and themselves that they have a better way or that they don't have to consider life insurance now. We all have a file full of these humorous but sometimes pitiful examples of reverse salesmanship.

The simplest form of game is squirming. We all know these symptoms: telephone hang ups, stand ups on appointments, cancellations of appointments, stalls until after Christmas, New Years, summer, winter, President's Day, etc. Consider some of these more intricate and one-upsmanship games. Some are the clients; some are the salesmen's.

1. I made a sale to a client on the basis of converting his personal term insurance and assigning it to his profit sharing plan. The conversion application was completed at his office but he told me the policy itself was at home. He indicated he would mail it to me that night. I gave him an envelope addressed to me. A week went by and the policy didn't come, so I called him on the phone. He apologized and said he would send it as soon as he got home. Another week went by and I called him again. He said he forgot it and would get it out that night. After I suggested that I stop by his home to pick up the policy, he firmly assured me there was no need to do that and I would have the policy in a few days. I suggested that if it was lost, I could get a lost policy form but he said, "I just have to get it out of the box." Another two weeks went by and I didn't get the policy. I really thought he was brushing me off in stages. When I called him again he said, "I still haven't gotten it out of the box."

I asked, "Are you speaking of a safety deposit box?"

He said, "No, the shoe box in my closet."

2. "The check is in the mail."

3. I have more than one client who plays the grace period game. I realize that we all have people who pay on the last day of grace but I have one client who has told me that, "When I die I want to get the most out of my insurance; I want to owe the insurance company money." This certainly shows another plus for the flexibility of our product. Let this man try this trick by passing the due date of his bank note by 31 days. There would be no "grace" in the banker's phone call and the interest penalty piled on.

4. I play games, too, as I think all of us do. I already illustrated some of my proposals. I make these to keep myself challenged and have some fun while I'm working. On some occasions, when I have to do a proposal, I complete the whole thing but without the premium. I explain everything except the premium. When the client asks, "What does it cost?" I ask, "What's it worth to you?"

5. When you have lost round one of the term versus permanent fight and you have applied for a term policy, try what I did as shown by Il-

Illustration 6-1

*** POLICY SPECIFICATIONS ***

DATE OF ISSUE Dec 6 1977

AGE 34

INSURED James A ---------

FACE AMOUNT	$100000
FIRST EXPIRY DATE	Sep 3 1981
FINAL EXPIRY DATE	Sep 3 2012
CONVERSION PERIOD	31 Years
POLICY DATE	Sep 3 1976
POLICY NUMBER	----------
POLICY CLASS	Standard

SCHEDULE OF BENEFITS AND PREMIUMS

BENEFIT		Yearly Premium
BASIC POLICY	or $1872.00	$337.00

EXPIRY DATE		Yearly Premiums On Renewal
Sep 3 1981	1504.00	$427.00
Sep 3 1986	1209.00	$618.00
Sep 3 1991	1051.00	$937.00
Sep 3 1996	884.00	$1420.00
Sep 3 2001	754.00	$2214.00
Sep 3 2006	604.00	$3512.00
Sep 3 2011	454.00	$4540.00

EQUITY	58,100	0
Total Premiums	41,680	65,485

lustration 6-1. In this case I showed a 34 year old attorney a $100,000 permanent contract. We had the usual joust on term versus permanent and he won. So I ordered the term policy. What you see in Illustration 6-1 is the front page of the term policy. The printed numbers are obviously the renewable term rates; the lettered numbers were written by me. I explained that there were two kinds of term; one with increasing premium, the other with decreasing premium. I showed the total premiums to age 65. These are labeled "Total Premiums." I also showed the cash values labeled "Equity." I didn't do much selling. All I said was, "Here is your policy" as I showed the term rates. "Or, you can have these rates and equity."

He said, "Why didn't you show me the decreasing rates in the first place?" So he took the permanent alternate I had ordered and I sent back the term policy with the writing on page one. So far, the companies haven't complained about the writing on the policies.

Think what has gone on in this game. I did what I thought was my best and couldn't place the permanent. Then, almost backhandedly, I toss off the idea of "either, or", and he wants it his way. Not only that but he blames it on me. I guess I lost the communication game here. But we'll play this one again.

6. The "Same To You" Game

At the 1975 Million Dollar Round Table meeting in San Francisco, I was walking from the Hyatt to one of the meetings at the main convention building. There was one block on the way that housed a number of sauna bath houses, topless bars and other self-proclaimed fun houses. In front of one of these places there was a tall, thin dude dressed in a maroon cutaway tuxedo with gold fringe and a top hat. He was stunning but looked like bad news.

As I approached, he stepped in front of me and said, "No cover charge, just go in m' man." I said, "No thanks," and tried to edge my way around him. He moved squarely in front of me and persisted, almost grabbing me by the shoulder and steering me towards the front door. He was selling hard. I said to him, "I'm here with the insurance convention. I'm an insurance salesman and I'd like to talk to you about $100,000 of twenty-year endowment."

He protested, "I can't afford it, man."

I countered, "My story exactly, excuse me." And I stepped around him.

Since then, I have used that approach many times when I have been solicited by vendors on the street or those who manage to corner me in shopping centers or get into our office building. When they won't accept my "no" answer I say, "I'd love to talk to you further about this. How about making an appointment or come on up to my office now. I want to talk about your life insurance needs." I consistantly don't make any sales by this approach but my counterpart salesperson quickly backs off.

7. The Raffle Ticket Insurance Sale

Let me tell you of an incident which exemplifies the three basic forms of competition we have. This episode will show the tenacious and, at the same time, pitiful competition that we face.

A policeman came into our office one day selling $1.00 tickets for a field day or drawing of some sort. He poked his head into my office and asked if I wanted to buy a ticket for "a buck." It's tough to say "no" to the law and also embarrassing to refuse a direct approach for only "a buck." But I did ask him what the dollar would do. He explained the dangerous job of a police officer and that some men died in the line of duty. The fund which would be created by the sale of these tickets would allow for a $1,000 death payment to policemen killed in the line of duty.

He tried to do some hard selling, hoping that I might buy two tickets. He explained that widows and orphans were placed in a financial bind. I mentioned to him that in that regard, he and I were in the same business. I asked if he knew he could buy $1,000 of widows and orphans benefits for about $20.00 per year. He said he couldn't afford it. At this point I decided I would not buy a ticket from him since I didn't believe in the type of insurance being perpetuated by policemen who were collecting a debit on their off-duty hours. He wasn't too pleased with me and probably thought I was some kind of smart aleck.

The policeman couldn't see the logic of buying cash value full-time insurance as opposed to the soul-cleansing benevolence of a fund collected dollar by dollar. He really thought his method was more efficient and better than ours. He would rather rely on the three kinds of competition I mentioned previously—*chance, luck or charity*.

8. The "Stall to a Higher Level" Game

Here is the case of Al D. Al happens to be the uncle of one of my former associates in the Detroit area. He was, therefore, very easily approachable. Al was reported to be very wealthy and constantly complaining to any family member who would listen that taxes were taking too much of his income. I didn't think he had heard the estate tax story yet so I called him. We had an interview and he was very interested in doing something about the estate tax shrinkage on his death. We figured his taxes to be over $100,000 at the first death and greater at the second death, unless some conservation or shifting of the burden was done. He owned about $5,000 of life insurance and it had taken 51 years of his life to get up to that sizable sum. When I suggested a premium of $4,000 for the $100,000 of insurance, he naturally balked. After a considerable number of serves and returns, Al agreed to a $1,000 premium for $25,000 of permanent insurance. I wasn't happy with this partial solution so I thought I would attempt to get him some insurance through a tax deductible retirement plan. However, I wasn't going to do anything until we delivered the $25,000 policy.

Al's business situation was this. He was a self-employed painting contractor who hired between a high of 30 painters and a low of 18. He had been in business for 16 years. He was contributing $32 per painter, per week, to the union pension fund for his painters but still had no retirement fund for himself.

Since he was self-employed the only thing he could opt for was the HR-10 plan. On delivery of the $25,000 policy, I showed him a proposal for a HR-10. He said the $7,500 deduction was not enough. I suggested the only way to go higher was to incorporate. His answer to this was that he had thought of it many times before. He asked that I research the possibilities of a plan with the IRS. I visited the IRS and got advance approval for a corporate plan, excluding all members of a collective bargaining unit. Al was the only other employee so we drew the plan with a 10-year past-service liability, which meant he owed the participants $60,000 and could fund this over the next 14 years. Since he was the only participant this meant he could put away $10-12,000 a year. When I called Al on the phone to give him the news of the IRS visit, he was ecstatic. But that was the last happy note in this case. It took a gigantic three hour interview to strike out. The plan actually would cost him zero because of his tax bracket, but I couldn't close it and to this day he's done nothing.

9. The "Can't Look You in the Eye" Game

Here is the story of Mr. B.V. Bernie was a policyholder of ours who owned $10,000 of Pension at 65. He was a 45-year old builder who was doing extremely well. From the application for the $10,000 policy, I knew he owned no other insurance. I had an estate planning interview with him at which he told me his net worth was over $500,000 and his annual income was $125,000. He also showed me his marital trust document. I gathered information and told him I would be back in a week or so with an analysis. When we met again, I showed him my report with the recommendation that he buy $100,000 of permanent insurance. He agreed with the reasoning but wanted his lawyer to check my work and meet me. I set up a meeting with the lawyer. He agreed with me. I asked him if he would give me a note to Bernie saying so. He took out one of his calling cards and wrote on the back that he felt Bernie should buy at least the $100,000 policy and probably twice that much. I was happy. I had done everything right. I analyzed the case, got the lawyer and client on my side, and had a note to the client from the lawyer in whom the client had complete faith. I called Bernie to set up an appointment for the following week. I got the date and Bernie stood me up. I called him and he made an excuse about the construction crew and said he would call me. I tried many times after that but for the last two years I've never seen Bernie. He gave me a first-class runaround. I suppose he thinks he won the game.

10. The "Reverse of Roles" Game

We've all had this happen one way or another but I always get a kick out of these situations. I dealt with a corporation for nine months trying to complete a stock redemption case. There were four shareholders. Three of them were easy to deal with and the other let it be known that he just didn't care about or believe in insurance. After the sale was closed and we were involved in the underwriting and issuing procedure, I had an urgent phone call from my dissident shareholder. "I'm going on a trip next week and I want to be sure my insurance is in force," he said.

An offshoot of this game is the policyholder who resists buying and in general is a tough prospect who finally buys. Then he is on the phone the day after the medical asking, "How did I do? Will I get my insurance?"

11. The No Need Game

I had the following situation twice in one year. Two young wives, both in their thirties, died. Both husbands called me a short while later to lapse their own policies. They were very sad and indicated they had no beneficiaries. One man did have children and the other didn't but in neither case could I make enough of an impact to conserve the policies. Both subsequently remarried. One set up a program again; the other didn't.

12. The Bragging Game

In this game, salesmen increase their volume every half-hour just by talking about it. I've been guilty of it myself and I guess we all do it. It's part of the ego syndrome. Someone once said to me that there was more insurance sold in bars than any other single locale.

I was talking to a first time attendee at one of the Million Dollar Round Table meetings and he told me that he felt grossly inadequate and out of place. He said all he heard about were million dollar sales and hundred thousand dollar premiums. All he had done was the 1.25 million that was required to make the 1978 meeting. I told him that I always discounted production by a third when other agents were too quick and too free to offer numbers. I told him at MDRT meetings it was even appropos to reduce volume by one-half.

At company meetings or conventions it's a little harder to escalate the figures too high since there is usually a production honor roll or roster. The fanciful agent has to switch gears and talk about items that can't be verified so we get that wildly, "let your imagination be your guide" category called "Outside Business." This "surplus" line ain't so easily checked.

I have to admit that when I go to meetings and see some of my colleagues looking sharp and exuding airs of confidence and success, I sometimes feel that I'm doing something wrong. When I see two of them talking energetically, I think they're talking about girls. When I see three of them pawing the ground for territorial position and listening fast so they don't miss the other guy's pause so they can jump in, I think they're talking about forming their own company. If collectively we produced half the volume we proclaim we do, we could pay off the national debt in just one year from that growing cesspool called "unassigned surplus."

13. The Conscientious Objector Game

On only a few occasions have I had people object on "religious" grounds. I never knew of any religions that forbade life insurance but it's tough to refute this kind of objection. I always felt I had to take this kind of response seriously because I didn't want to be sacrilegious, especially when the prospect was being so serious.

I once had a client who was of a particular denomination that didn't believe in doctors or medicine. He had no objection to life insurance but he wouldn't get medically examined. On the first occasion we met I sold him the maximum non-medical limits available. The non-medical form only stated his height, weight and the state of health of parents, brothers, and sisters; all good as you might suspect. Everything else was "no"; he had never been sick.

His status in life indicated a great need and he would have bought whatever the fact-finding showed, but he wouldn't get examined. A few years later when the non-medical limits changed, I called him and he bought the maximum. Again a few years later, he took all that was available on the increased limits. He died of a heart attack about two months after he bought the last policy.

The check for the first two policies came in prompt fashion, along with a note that the third policy was being investigated. I wondered what there was to investigate because there was absolutely no medical history whatever. If he had had chest pains or high blood pressure or complained about anything else, who could prove anything? He simply had never had any professional help or advice. Apparently, the claims department had the same feelings because their investigation took only one day. The check arrived the day afterward. Bob was 45 when he died. I often wonder if an insurance medical would have shown symptoms and stimulated him to seek treatment. His wife, Mary, has purchased the maximum non-medical insurance allowable for her age and the beat goes on.

As I said, I always had problems with the religious objection so I really gave it some thought in one particular situation and came up with a logical conclusion to the problem. I had inherited an orphan client who owned an extremely small amount of insurance. When I had the appointment I found a thriving construction business owned completely by this man. His income was deep into six figures and his estate was deep into seven figures. During the interview, I suddenly found myself on the receiving end of a conversion lecture. He wanted me to change my religion to his. I tried to be polite and tolerant but I didn't want to discuss changing faiths. I did want to get back on the track of changing the estate make up in favor of the client and away from the government taxing system. (Is this what you might call not intermingling Church and State?)

He was fervent and after a long meeting the best I could do was get the census for a pension plan. He didn't feel that a little tax deductible insurance would be too bad. I came back with the plan and presented it. Not too long into the appointment we were back into the discussion of my religion. I got the meeting back to tax and estate planning but the whole emphasis shifted again when the client took the approach that, "The Lord will provide. He didn't put me on earth to cause problems for my family. If He takes me, He knows what He is doing and He will take care of them." The client was so intense that I was happy to get out of that meeting and just call it a strikeout.

About a year later, when I saw this man's name in my file, I sincerely felt that planning was an absolute necessity, so I geared myself up and made another appointment. There was no problem in getting the meeting; he was happy to have another shot at me. I gave that interview a tremendous amount of preparatory brain-storming time because I genuinely felt there was a dire need. I just had to find the key, and it wasn't numbers. I came up with what I thought was the key. The interview went just as I thought it would and provided me with the all-time answer for these types of situations.

Not too long into the meeting, he took over the salesman's pulpit and started, "The Lord will provide" sermon. I asked why he owned the little bit of insurance he did. He answered, "Because it was respectable. People feel that you shouldn't leave your family out in the cold and I don't want to be criticized later."

I said to him, "Jack, you're right in saying the Lord will provide. I think He has. Do you know something? I didn't invent life insurance. Think back to your Bible when Pharoah instructed Joseph to take up "the fifth part of the land" because there would be seven plenteous years and seven famine years. And the people survived because there was food and stores for the dearth years. This wasn't computers, contracts, policies, cash values, loan provisions, home offices, agents, etc. This was pure and simple life insurance. It was seven pay life with a seven year settlement option. Life insurance exists today not because the agents or companies want it; it exists because the people want it. With over 250 years of commercial experience, if it was in any way in conflict with people's beliefs, it would have disappeared. Among the policyholders of the industry are the most religious people in the world. The non-caring heathens don't buy this product; those who truly care do."

He agreed to see my attorney for a will and trust. He bought the minimum insurance required by the estate calculations. I think he's happier but he never showed any emotion or tried to proselyte me after that.

Time out!!

7

Games People Play — Second Half

Some of games people play are done as substitutes. Consider this story:

1. Just for one moment let's think of the product we are selling. We think that it really is insurance, and along with that, we come up with the idea that this insurance is the solution to problems. Therefore, too many of us sometimes zero in immediately on the solution without creating the problem.

I was in the office of one salesman whom I respect very much and saw one of the best jobs of selling the problems, or selling the needs, that I have ever seen in my life. And the result was that the client very enthusiastically was desiring the solution and he quickly said, "I can see where I need some more liquidity on my wife and, therefore, I probably should buy some more insurance on her. Along with that, I probably should buy some more on myself."

The client was very enthusiastic about getting the insurance, but the salesman continued to establish the problems by saying, "That's one way of solving the problem, and all I'm doing is exposing your liability." The result was a $200,000 sale; $150,000 on the wife, and $50,000 on the husband.

Now, the upshot of the story is that the man who was the salesman really wasn't selling insurance or selling problems at all. What he was selling was wills and trusts. As it turned out, this was a meeting at which I had some clients and the attorney was selling his services. For the two wills and two trusts involved, he charged $950, which was a fair rate for the work that he was going to do. Truthfully, however, this was the only item that he was concerned with, the items for which he was getting paid. But he did exactly what we should be doing in our work, and that is selling the problems . . . and the solution becomes almost natural.

The client, in this case, wanted the solution so much that the proper legal documents and the insurance applications were taken right there and the examinations set up. I repeat, know what you are selling, and it is not the solution, it is the problem.

Along with that I advise you, wherever possible, to use the best possible professional help you can. Learn to get along with lawyers, C.P.A.'s, bank officers, and anyone else who can help you in their particular field, and use them in the proper context. Sometimes you won't get along with all of them. For the most part, however, you will not beat them by fighting them, so learn to get along with them and make them look as if they are in the driver's seat if that is what's necessary.

2. The Real Name of the Game

The scene is a high-rise apartment on the riverfront in downtown Detroit. An estate sale is taking place. There is great activity going on. The bargains are real and activity brisk. Members of the family were handling the sale and were anxious to have all of the furniture and personal effects sell quickly so that too much time wasn't taken in finalizing the closing of the apartment.

Off to one side another drama was unfolding. One customer had her eye fixed on a certain side credenza which she loved and thought would fit perfectly in her home. The problem was the price. She was agonizing over whether or not her budget could stand this piece of furniture. Should she or shouldn't she? Other customers looked at this item. She became panicky. She better, but no, the price, although reduced, was too much for her. She labored for an hour or longer before she decided she would buy it. But she couldn't afford the price tag all at once so she had to muster up the courage to ask for time payments. However, this isn't unusual in sophisticated estate sales. To her amazement the seller said to her, "Evelyn, you *can't* have time payments—we want you to have the credenza. Take it free."

Careful thinking about price wasn't unusual, but the "free" offer was. So let's examine the circumstances a little more closely: The high-rise apartment was the Allan Towers, a senior citizen retirement building in downtown Detroit. Top rent $110 per month, and many of these people are subsidized by the government. I'm familiar with the estate because it was my mother's. The credenza in question was being sold for $15 and the buyer was a 70-year old neighbor existing on Social Security of under $200 per month.

The finale to the story is that we wanted to give her the credenza saying that my mother would have wanted her to have it. Evelyn wouldn't take it on that basis so we arranged for payments on the $15. Ultimately, she called that night and said she couldn't afford it, so it went to someone else.

Now, let's relate this to our business. Think about the "estate planning," "deferred compensation," "retirement plans," "advanced underwriting," and all other forms of utopian ideas that materialize on that magic retirement day. I don't know what this lady's financial status was. I don't know if her husband was well-to-do or not, or what kind of estate he left or didn't leave. All I know is that I saw an old lady trying to justify a $15 installment purchase because she didn't have the money. Just pause and think about that for a minute or so the next time you pitch $.75 or $.80 or whatever into a cigarette machine and watch the money go up in smoke. This lady's situation was not unusual. I watched old people thinking hard as to whether or not they should buy eight pieces of silverware or nine at a price of a dime each. Also, think of these poor people when their young counterparts say, "I can't afford it," "the government will take care of me," "I'm going to get an inheritance," "I've got group insurance," "my wife works," and all other forms of defensive, salesmanship testing, unthinking, and baloney objections. You and I have an obligation to the small buyer just as we have an obligation to the big buyer. And if enough of us don't fulfill it, the government will.

3. The "What Kind of Fool am I" Game.

Every salesman has had a variation of this game but this example goes above and beyond. I did an interview with a young couple in their thirties who had three children. The husband owned a leather goods business and made a substantial living. The interview was done at their home. I talked about estate tax and he was fully aware of it because when his father died certain assets had to be sold to pay the balance due. The husband had heard about flower bonds and wished his father's estate would have had some so the burden would have been lessened.

The client's estate was made-up chiefly of the leather business and raw land awaiting future development. The client owned a small amount of life insurance and had no will or trust. I felt, given all these circumstances, he was an ideal candidate for estate liquidity insurance.

The analysis showed a great need for insurance. During the course of the interview the wife cried because no one else had ever invited her to sit in on an interview and she didn't realize how much her husband was worth and what the consequences of no planning would be. I tried to get an application that night but he resisted by saying he wanted to do one thing at a time and primary to him was a meeting with a lawyer whose name he had just gotten. Then we would meet again. The lawyer's name was familiar to me and I knew he was a good estate planner. I tried a medical close but Joe insisted on seeing the lawyer first. Given all the facts of the case, and the $300,000 shortage of liquidity, I wasn't too uncomfortable with the fact that we could do the work in two stages but only if he did not delay and actually saw the attorney. He promised me that he would. On the way out of the house, the wife thanked me over and over again for having this meeting. She also shed a few more tears. The husband thanked me profusely and wanted to show me his new Mercedes. It was nice.

The next day, I made a note in my calendar to call him back in two weeks. However, he called me that day and said he already had a meeting with the lawyer. I offered to accompany him but he wanted to go alone. A week later he called me and said the will and trust were being drawn up but the lawyer said he could arrange the estate so there would be no taxes. It was unbelievable. There was no way, unless the assets Joe listed with me were not accurate. I asked him if the attorney had the same set of circumstances that I did and he said, "Yes." He also assured me that he could not have afforded the premium on the insurance I had shown, but in any event he didn't need it.

He asked me to send him a bill for time and services rendered but I refused because that was not the basis on which we started our dealings. I also told him I was quite happy if he was happy, that at least he had taken one part of my advice and had gotten to the attorney for documents. He insisted on sending me a fee but I told him no. Later, he called my house to once again offer a fee payment, but I refused.

That night he called again and said, "At least let my wife and me take you and Sharon out to dinner." I refused that also. Later that evening his wife called Sharon and said they were appreciative of the help I had given him and they wanted to "please take you out to dinner." Sharon and I discussed it and I finally agreed. They picked us up on the appointed night in a different colored Mercedes than the one I had previously seen. When I asked if he had traded cars, he said, "No, I bought this one for her."

4. The Ego Game

This is one we salesmen play with ourselves. We put on our cards all kinds of super-duper selling clubs, presidents' clubs, honor clubs, etc. The companies honor us with titles and little kudos of bragadocia. The greatest honor we could have as a high schooler was a letter sweater. We proved we had been to war and we were victorious. In the insurance business, it's the plaque. On occasion the plaque can become the plague. They won't stop. After a while, they become meaningless. In some bad production year, I'd rather have the plaque rights in my territory than the insurance rights. We've all heard the story of the birth of the insurance business; it was founded by an unemployed paper salesman, an unemployed doctor, and an out-of-work plaque salesman.

The designs and figures some of us make on our walls with these trophies are an art form unto themselves. The trophies themselves range from hideous to beautiful. They become so bountiful in some places that they are without significance. Full walls have been covered and even the smallest office can have a "wall of fame." I have a total of 364 plaques, ranging from "Leading Agent" to "Best Attendance Award for a Unit Trainee." I only keep three of the most meaningful in my office. The others are kept in my basement and have survived moves by some of the biggest van lines and the ablest of teamsters. I do appreciate them and have a ritual of looking at them each New Years Day. This is a time when the production meters are set back to zero and I need something to convince me that I'm still a potent force in the sales wars.

One year, after counting them, I was sure one was missing. My wife assured me that it was only a certificate and not a plaque that I got for being runner-up in the "1976 Cashier's Leap Year Production Regatta." I still think one of our cleaning ladies took it. If she had asked I would have given her one. I'm not stingy and she probably deserves it for dusting all the others. I can prove that I think these monuments are worthy and can spread the gospel of meritorious service. The following is a true story of the value of the stroking effect of the prizes.

In 1977, Bill Clancey, CLU, and I were setting up offices in Troy,

Michigan. The furniture was all in place and we were trying to get unpacked and start working. I was at my desk shuffling papers as every good salesman should. Right behind me was my credenza and right behind it was the telephone man. He had been there for quite awhile and two thoughts had crossed my mind. One, he must have been the trainer for the prisoners we see in war newsreels; he could squat for the longest time. Secondly, it was two in the afternoon and I thought he was playing out the job so he wouldn't have to report back to the central office for another assignment. Every so often he would talk to somebody on one of those rusty, dirty, internal workings of a phone instrument which he had strapped to his waist.

The United Parcel man had just been in the outer office and my secretary came into my office with a big square package which could only have been one thing—No. 365. The telephone man peeked his head out from behind the credenza and I heard his knees crack so I knew he was standing up. He leaned over the back of my chair as I took a letter opener and sliced open the parcel. As usual, the shredded rag content paper fell all over me and the desk and the chair. The telephone man said, "That's terrible. People don't got no pride in their work no more." But he was excited and happy for me as I took out this beautiful mahogany, bronze, black felt award. He said, "That's nice." A thought struck me. I said, "Doesn't the phone company give you trophies for good work?"

"Naw," he said. "We don't get nuthen like that."

"That's rotten," I responded. "I'll tell you what, you finish this job in fifteen minutes and I'll give you this plaque."

He looked puzzled and said, "It's got your name on it."

I told him, "You've got two ways to fix it. One, you can go to a bowling trophy shop and get your name engraved on a plate, or, two, you can put tape over my name and letter yours in." His eyes blinked like the dials on two "hold" buttons.

"You're kidding," he said. I saw he was motivated.

"Nope."

He saw I was serious and jumped back behind the credenza. I wish I would have had my Casio stopwatch on him but I would swear it was no longer than twenty seconds when he stood up and said, "Wanna give me a hand pushing back the furniture?"

Never let the power of a plaque be underestimated. As he floated out of the office with the plaque under one arm and lugging his tool kit in the other, the monument had done double duty; he was happy and so was I.

In June 1978, we were moving into larger offices in Birmingham, Michigan. The place was a mess because the remodeling was not yet done and the telephone men were coming in on the same day. You guessed it, who walks in the door but my "Leading Producer of 1977." He was delighted to see me but no more than I because I knew we were going to get good service. He said, "I remember you. You gave me the prize last year." I asked what he had done with it and he told me that he had used the tape covering method with his name lettered on. The plaque was hung in his family room. I must admit there was evil in my voice as I said, "Want another plaque?"

5. The Time On My Hands Game

One of the elements we always fight is "time." We have heard expert testimony that there are only 24 hours in a day, 168 hours in a week, 60 minutes in an hour, etc. There are many ways to spend time or waste it. We have also heard that one man can do more in a day than another man, even though there are no differences in schedules.

Various articles and services are for sale concerning time control. They talk about "the 23 time wasters" and "time for sale." Let me tell you, I'm guilty of all of them, and if there's a 24th method, I'm guilty of that, too. And, you know what, I don't care. The reason being that for myself, I don't consider all of these common "time wasters" as waste. I take no exception with the articles and all of the materials one could buy concerning time control. I think they're great. I think they're necessary, for almost everyone. I think all of us could stand improvement in many areas of our operations. But please don't take my remarks as an attack on hard-hitting scheduled work with the meter running all day.

I also make no attack on all the services one could buy to pack more selling time into the same 24 hours which we're all allotted. For me, I can do more in eleven months than I can in twelve. I can do more in seven hours a day than I can in ten. I can do more with frequent phone interruptions and drop-in visitors. I believe there are many people, just like myself, who have short bursts of great energy, but need frequent breaks in between. Truthfully, I wilt under the burden of a regimented, hectic schedule. I don't believe I do justice to any one thing when I'm under pressure. Fortunately for me, I can think of more than one thing at once; so when an associate drops into my office to talk about Jacques

Cousteau's jaws, I can easily be sweeping my mind clear for my next project while I'm engaged in non-headache type talk.

All of this doesn't mean that I don't have any schedule; I do, and by some standards it might be considered busy. But *I* don't think it is, so I breeze but don't squeeze at my work. One of my favorite expressions is, "What difference will it make ten years from now?" Once again I caution you: this philosophy works for me and may be contrary to your method or your supervisor's projected method of work for you. But I make no reservations about the statement that I'm trying to appeal to your place in the sun as an individual. Like the kids say, "Do your own thing . . . but you've got to know what it is."

6. The Slump Game

Let's talk about futures . . . isn't that a great thought? I have to give credit to the origination of that line. I play a lot of racquetball as some of you know. In fact, I've been accused of having to leave the courts only to do some work and pay for the addiction. One day, three of us were in the locker room after we had finished playing. My friend, Carl Brettschneider was kidding Ken Wilson, who was the big loser that day—Kenny had played untypically bad; he just had an off day. To counter Carl's jokes and get the losses in the past he said, "Let's talk about the future."

A simple phrase, but doesn't it say a lot? All of us have been in slumps from time to time, self-imposed or otherwise. Most times it isn't our fault. It's the manager's, the economy, or the service work, or the government, or the underwriting department, your family's, sun spots, or the bomb. However, no matter whose fault it is, what's the difference? It's normal to have slumps. We all get them. So don't worry too hard when they come; ride them out. They pass and they only mean that you're on target with other salesmen. But like the Dow-Jones, for every slump there is a crest, and hopefully, each peak is taller than the one before.

All we have to talk about is the future. We all know it's tough to exist on renewals only, so where is our income coming from? New business, and where is the new business? In the future!! If you've had some rough spots, forget them. They're past. Let's talk about futures. And when you're talking about futures, don't try to recoup your losses from slumps too fast. Steady, solid, building recovery is needed. Incidentally, a slump is a good time to accomplish busy work. Bring your files up-to-date. Catch up on reading. Take your manager to lunch.

Punish yourself if you want and start your diet. But it's your slump, no one elses—enjoy it. Maybe you won't have another one for quite a while. Slumps also serve another purpose—they balance off big heads from jumbo sales.

I'll give you one tip on how to work your way out of a slump. At least it works well for me. When things aren't going well, promise yourself to make enough calls each day to set up one future interview. Just one. But if you set up one a day, eventually you conduct one a day and this activity will start you moving. But you can only set up one a day; remember, you're in a slump! No full day's calling to set up a full week. Just one a day—then quit. If you get your appointment on the first call, your calling for the day is done. If it takes twenty calls, do it. Constant activity does amazing things. I sincerely believe a $10,000 sale can cure a cold and a $15,000 sale can get rid of the flu. Any size application gets rid of many assorted imagined ailments, and a $50,000 sale can grow hair.

To summarize this point on slumps and futures, there are three things that generate a positive attitude, and they are in alphabetical order . . . activity . . . activity . . . and activity.

By taking positive action it will help clear the air and get the fuzz out of your brain. If you can't sell something, buy something. Spend ten bucks on a tie, or in my case as an athlete, I improve my game, looks, and spirits by buying a tennis shirt. When the season-end markdown sales start, some of the sports shops call on me to buy back my stock. I have a greater assortment than some of them do.

7. The "Anything You Can Do" Game

What does it take to be a successful salesperson? It takes a lot of elements to make the right combination, but the proportion of each is different for each person. I'm going to comment on some of the ingredients. I do believe the chief ingredient is *desire*. Somehow a salesman has to *desire* to succeed in his particular goal. I allude to the seduction process. Consider for a moment the *desire* going on here, for both parties. One party is saying "No," all the time meaning "Yes" with some small degree of desire. The other party is being dominant, all the time having a great desire. When the deal is consummated, both parties are happy. If a salesman could sell insurance with the same concentration needed to sell sex, he'd succeed fantastically.

One doesn't have to be the best dresser in the world. Today, anything goes in clothes. We recently had a very successful C.P.A. in our office who wore a Levi suit and carried a large purse as a briefcase. Look around today at the spectrum of clothes from bankers gray to sports outfits. You'll also see necklaces, bracelets, and maybe an earring or two . . . on the men.

The answer doesn't come in from hard work. Some agents have to have hundreds of prospects. Some can operate on very few. Some must do tremendous numbers of interviews, some get by on one or two a week and do extremely well. Some set up regular forms of prospecting through lists, clubs, and other methods. Others do no prospecting but can exist out of their own files or a rare name they get as a referral. Some do a big business by great numbers of small policies in the family or young person's market. Some do a large business with one sale per month. Some specialize in one form of advanced underwriting, some specialize in no one form but do a mixed business; some "specialize" in everything, and their business card will tell you so. One doesn't have to be the best educated person in the world. We've probably got some PhD's in the business and we have many high school dropouts.

What the magic common denominators are, I don't know. What works for one person will be a strain for another. I'll tell you what I think some of the ingredients are: honesty, sincerity, hard work, creativity, interest in your clients needs, patience, service and as much knowledge as your individual body will handle.

This last factor mentioned is important—individuality. I can't do what some of you do and all of you can't do what I do. We can listen to what some of the successful people in the industry do and take those items which are adaptable and transferable. But none of us can duplicate the other guy. Therefore, one of the things a good salesman should lack is **jealousy**. Know thyself, the big ratebook says. Don't long for such unreachable goals that you can't attain the proper ones for you. This may seem like a somewhat reactionary view but a lot of failures in our business never really gave themselves a chance. They only missed their own target because they never saw it. They saw the beacon light which drew them onto the rocks. And that was someone else's goals. Forget all that baloney. You're an individual. There is only one like you in the whole world. Do what you do . . . well!

I remember when I was a member of a school board. We used to have classes for "retarded" children. We thought that was a little blunt so we changed it to "special education" but everyone still knew what that was. So we changed it to "exceptional children." Now, no one can tell if this is a kid with a problem or some genius gobbling up grades two at a time. I say the same to each of you individually. You're **exceptional**. There ain't no one else on earth **except** you who is just like you. So do the very best with what you got and do it proudly.

8. The "What Goes Up . . ." Game

I've had my winners and I've had my losers. God bless the losers. We need an inter-sprinkling of them to have enough winners. I don't set goals in number of prospects. I just work hard every day. I get up every day at 6:00 am and I'm at the office by 7:30-7:45 am, which is a little later than I'd like. I'm a morning person and I wind down at night. I probably do only one evening appointment per month. I spend a lot of time with my kids and I like television so I stay home most nights and many Saturday nights. I play ball every day at lunch time. I don't like business lunches. I probably had three of those all last year. I don't function well with waiters, dishes, dropover guests, etc. My client has a business place and so do I, so we meet for business and I keep taking rain checks on lunches. Besides, I watch my weight and I like to eat an orange after a workout.

One of the traps of this business is that there is no way of knowing how high is up. I really do work to pace myself down. Life is only so long. None of us have to look very far among friends, relatives, clients, or associates to see the heart attacks, ulcers, breakdowns, family problems, kids with narcotics, and so on. To cure many of these, you can't use money; you've got to apply time in liberal doses. This means saying "Yes" to some things such as an evening playing Monopoly with the kids or helping them with homework, and "No" to one more committee meeting. Temperence is needed, though, because you want to say "Yes" uptown when your child wants piano lessons, or college out of state, or social flu gets you and you want a bigger house or car. To do this you have to say "No" downtown to a longer lunch, to the lazy bug when he says the phone isn't working today so don't make any more calls, "No" to knocking off early when your stomach says, "It ain't right." I can take the steam out of a lot of psychiatrists action by simply stating that balance is necessary. This also means saying "Yes" to your wife when she asks you to pick something up from the store. I pick up the cleaning when necessary and I take my own car in for service. I don't ever want to become so much of a robot that I haven't got time to be human. I don't want to be a selling machine.

So I say to you, "do less . . . at the right time" and "do more . . . at the right time.'' Your built-in computer, which is your stomach and not your brain, will tell you when you have an overload or an underload. Work to capacity but within your own limitations. A little progress, steadily each year, will astound you. But big eyes for the MDRT, then life membership, then company leadership, world leadership, and in the age of rockets, being the biggest salesman on the moon will hurt you if the launch is faulty. We're all individuals; be honest with yourself, appraise what you have and where you are. If you're truly a happy, well-balanced person, cherish it and work to preserve what you have. If you're truly unhappy, go to your church or your synagogue, or your parents, or your manager, or your gym or wherever else you're honest with yourself and start to improve slowly. Instant improvement is like instant coffee. It still takes time to boil the water.

Another Time out!!

8

Games People Play —Third Half

1. The Serious Game

Everyone promises. They promise service. They promise price. Promises were made to be broken. "A promise made is a debt unpaid." The insurance policy is a "bundle of rights" but since most of those rights will be paid in the future, it is also a "bundle of promises."

One of the things we promise ourselves is to save money. The banker promises, "We're always available to help you," after you've established good credit. The insurance policy also makes these two promises. Let me relate to you a story where the insurance policy fulfilled its promise when the banker and the individual couldn't.

One morning I got a frantic phone call from a client whose young son had just had an eye accident. He was examined by a doctor who said a specialist in one very finite field was needed. The doctor required was in Boston, Massachusetts and the patient was in Michigan. The two doctors had already spoken on the phone and arrangements were made for the boy to go to University Hospital in Ann Arbor, Michigan.

The problem was that in those days, the father did not have major medical insurance and between the front money for the doctor to fly from Boston and the hospital deposit, he needed $1,500, fast. He didn't have it in savings so he called the banker who said he would require a loan application and committee approval. There were two problems here: time, and the possibility of a loan rejection.

The father was desperate when he called me. Pleadingly, he asked if he had any cash value in his policies. When I told him he had sufficient cash value, he asked how fast he could get the money because the family was ready to drive to Ann Arbor right away. The doctor from Boston was already on the way. I told him to hurry by the office on the way to the hospital and I would have the check.

Those were the days when the companies were still requiring loan forms and inspection of policies. I called the home office and they approved the issuance of the check only when the policy was inspected by me and the form signed. I told him to bring the policy but if he had forgotten it, I would have released the check anyway. As a matter of fact, if necessary I would have loaned him the money.

We see the insurance promise to pay, once again paid when necessary, without conditions and without variables. The operation was successful. The boy is now a man and has no eye problems. The loan has been repaid and the serious game of saving for later completed itself.

2. The Difference Game

All of us should try to be different from each other by trying to be better. At the same time we should try to be the same as the proven, honest gentlemen agents in our business. I believe there are only two things I offer that are any different than any of the rest of my colleagues; knowledge and service. If a client is trying to decide between two honest, knowledgable agents, he truly has a problem, but it's a win-win situation. The more things change the more they stay the same. But I do try to do the little things differently so that I make an impression and am remembered.

3. For years, I used business cards and calendars that had the company name and my name on it and nothing else. No phone number and no address. The normal reaction to this is, "How will they get in touch with you?" The actual experience has been fantastic. In the case of the business cards, when I hand one to a person, I immediate-

ly know what impression I made on this prospect. If they take the card and put it in their pockets without comment, I know I have made no impression and asking for the card was just a decelerating step. If, on the other hand, he asks, "Where can I reach you, what is your number?" I then ask, "Do you have a pen?" I then give the phone number. If he wants the address, I tell him that, too. He writes it on the card and I know that card means something to him. I've made an initial impression. The card stands a chance of survival because his scrawny handwriting means more to him than the best printing job in the world. I've gotten him involved and I know we've gone a little further than salesman-prospect status. We're on our way to a dialogue instead of a monologue.

With the calendars, there isn't much choice because these go out in the mail. The recipient has no chance to ask me what the phone number is. When he wants to get me and does not have my number recorded elsewhere, he goes to the calendar and the action starts. He has to take action and get involved to get in touch with me. You would think the client would forget the whole matter, but that's not the way it works. He goes to the phone book but can't find me under the insurance company listings. I don't have a business listing under my last name, only our assumed name. In the white pages I'm shown as Irwin B. Meisel even though in business I'm known as Burt Meisel. By the time he gets me he really wants me. The intensity has only helped; believe me it doesn't hurt.

Have you ever gone to a hardware store for a certain item only to find they were out of it? If it's not a vital item, it could be postoned till later. Why not forget it? Human nature won't let you. Your mind will start working on what other stores are close by and might have it. People like to complete their missions. I found they have not been upset when we finally talk after he had to use his brain for three or four minutes. But it sticks in his mind that I'm not overly accessible and I'm worthwhile reaching.

Another item which I do without is a pen. On closing some sales and completing the applications, I ask to borrow a pen. You would think this would slow the sales completion process but it doesn't. The client's response is, "Don't you have a pen?" I respond, "I think I do somewhere but may I use yours?" He gives it to me, all the time watching me because if it's a good pen he wants to be sure he gets it back. If it's a cheapie he needs it, otherwise he won't be able to have blue ink spots in his pocket. When I complete the application, we're partners; my paper, his pen, his ink. It takes some of the sting out of the sales process. Now when I hand him back his own pen and ask him to sign, he can't say, "No" to taking back his own pen. It works very smoothly.

Another "absent" idea I use is to give proposals with no premiums. If I use proposals at all, other than term-ordinary comparisons, I cut off the premium column. This takes the emphasis away from "how much" and puts it onto "how come." This way the needs are not at all overshadowed by the cost. I find it leads to more sincere discussions.

4. The "By Appointment Only" Game

When the young agent first comes into the business he is quickly taught that appointments mean sales. The law of averages will work to whatever degree is proper. The new agent is as happy about an interview as he is about a sale. And he should be. Consider the real estate agent who gets a listing. He covets the listing because it means he has an exclusive on that property. If it sells the commission is his. The same is true of the life insurance interview. Of course there can be problems from the time of interview and delivery of policy but the same is true in any sale in any field. So to start out the young agent will take any appointment at any time. Sometimes he doesn't even know what an interview is. He may very well consider any chance encounter, during which he has his business dress or his business attitude on, as an interview.

When I think about "by appointment only" I usually think about doctors. Let's trace the thoughts of the young physician from training to specialization. When the young medic is in residency or internship, hours don't mean a thing. Two and three day shifts are the normal work load. Then he goes out to face the world and if he opens an office of his own, only his name goes on the door. People come and it isn't too long before the young guy is very busy. But at first every phone call in gets an appointment. Harking back to the days of house calls, you can even imagine the phone ringing at three in the morning for the new doctor and he is very concerned about another human being's welfare. He might even shout out to his wife, "Honey, I've got a patient," and rush off into the night to administer to human needs.

A couple of years pass and the sign on his door says, "By Appointment Only." He's arrived. He's got it made. He's a corporation and has all the trappings of success. New patients must have sterling references to get in yet still may hear, "The doctor is not taking new patients." The sign on the door may well be changed to read, "By Disappointment Only" because the only way to get in is by someone else's cancellation or even death. Our doctor has gone full cycle to success and doesn't want to see anyone new.

Unfortunately, the life insurance man can never get filled up. He works by appointment only and they're tough to come by. At first, we take our interviews anytime we can get them. Night calls are the normal thing. Long days are common. Activity during the day is even a problem because most calls are family oriented and need both husband and wife. Most agents stay in this market throughout their careers. Many start their own fields of specialization and with that the night calls disappear. There is nothing wrong with that and the business market has to be served. The family market must be served, too, and the full line life insurance man concentrating on family insurance stands out as one of life's greatest humanitarians. If one man gives $10,000 to charity, he is considered a generous benefactor. But if another man sets up hundreds of $10,000 policies for families and, therefore, precludes the necessity for charity for these widows and children, is he not as much a benefactor?

I sometimes hear agents talk about doing all of their appointments in the office. I try but I don't know how I possibly could get all of the diverse prospects who are deeply involved in their own worlds to take time to come into my office for something about which, at first, they truly are not interested. I probably do about half my interviews in and half out of the office. But we can't let pride or stubborness get in the way of seeing enough prospects. The simple truth is that we have to make sufficient appointments, no matter where they are conducted.

Here is a humorous incident which tells the whole story. I talked to a client of mine on the phone who I could tell was in the midst of an elated mood. I asked him what the high was all about. He explained to me that he had an evening appointment. His business was furniture rental and he did all of his business in model apartments or homes, all during the day. No one in his industry worked nights, face to face. I asked why he was so ecstatic about the night appointment and he summed up everything in one phrase: "Business is Business."

He was right and the way to get it is by appointment only, whenever and however suits your style.

5. The Stretching Game

We all play this game and the companies play it with us. The campaigns and contests are really a silly way of getting us to do what we should be doing anyway. We all have made fun of some of the contests and maybe even considered them laughable. But the simple truth is that they work. There are 52 weeks in a year and one would suspect that in a major insurance company the production would be pretty evenly spaced. The law of averages works here, too. But I know of one agency who did 50 percent of its production in two campaigns consisting of 14 weeks total. The spring campaign was six weeks and the fall campaign eights weeks but half the production came in these periods that competition was going on. The companies give recognition to agents on lives, volume, interviews, consecutive weeks production, new man, experienced man status, etc. They come up with interim reports and pictures, small prizes, and a lot of hoopla. Silly, but it works.

All of us want to improve on our records. So we play little games with ourselves. We've always got a stretching exercise going on. Most often, it's a secret and we're the only ones that realize we're doing something out of the ordinary. But like diets, we've always got a new system working for getting more prospects or more sales. We're always reorganizing systems to better get ourselves into a better selling posture. Sometimes we make bets with each other for two reasons. One to attain a higher goal and the other to beat our competitor.

Last year I leased the latest model of a very expensive car. I already had the previous years so when I brought it home Sharon said, "What did you do with the other one? Have you made arrangements to sell it?" I told her I hadn't even thought about selling the old one but I had friends who were interested in it. She asked if we could afford this gas guzzling pig. I responded that we could but I had an idea. Immediately, Sharon said she knew what I was going to say and didn't want to hear it. That night at dinner the kids were very thrilled with Detroit's finest and wanted to know if they could drive it. Generally, happiness reigned. Then I discussed my idea.

A lesson in life we all know is to work extra hard for something you really want. I told the kids I was going to pay the lease payments by doing one extra interview each week. For a long while, I had not done any family interviews and I really wanted to do some for the reasons of knowing what the effect of inflation was on the average family and because these families certainly needed planning. Actually, I wanted to bring myself back to reality and at the same time pay for something extra.

I told my family that if I did one evening appointment per week I would make two sales in a month and this would pay for the car. That was a Wednesday evening and I immediately went to the white pages for phone numbers of old clients I hadn't seen in a while. I made three phone calls and got two appointments, one for that Friday night. The kids were now very interested in how these appointments went.

On Friday I met with a couple in their early forties. Their means were modest but there was a need for additional protection and savings. They set up a $15,000 whole life policy. When I got home, everyone was elated that I set up insurance for people who needed it and at the same time made half of the lease payment. For a long while after that I continued doing the evening appointments, but to be perfectly honest with you and myself, I didn't like the night work. But I had made a commitment.

Here's the solution I decided upon. I recommend it to agents who are trying to get out of the late night pattern. I now call a prospect and tell him I want to do a favor for three people. First, him, because I want to meet one evening to explain his insurance program and the effect inflation has on it. Second, his wife, because I'll explain the program to her and at the same time get her out of the house. Third, me, because I'm going to ask that they both meet me at my office right after his work, say 5:30 pm. I would take 45 minutes to one hour explaining the insurance. Then, I would suggest he takes her out to dinner. I tell him in that way he does me a favor by allowing me to do an appointment at the end of my working day yet be home in time for my dinner.

The results have been excellent. Everyone likes to do favors for everyone else. The key here has been the wife because she's anxious to finish the business and go out to dinner.

6. The Association Game

Our terms and phrases always come back to one idea because it seems the only solution is instant money. We come up with the abstraction called "intangible," known as life insurance. The visible tangible proof of the abstraction is called a policy. This is something we can see and feel and read but it truly isn't the idea known as life insurance. The complete process of life insurance means different things to different people for different purposes. Life insurance is as intangible as a driver's license or a marriage certificate. The plastic license is tangible but the right to drive itself is intangible. The paper marriage certificate is tangible, the state of being married is intangible.

The evolution of the item called the "hot button" is the thing that sets off the desire to have the insurance. Most times we know what the need is and we sell to it. The client himself also knows what the need is but he wants reinforcement, therefore we have to go through the seduction process known as selling. We have to push many buttons until we find the one that is hot and melts the way to the sale. But in the process of gathering data, making presentations, second and more interviews, meeting with advisors, and all the other details, we don't really know what triggered the decision to actually set up the insurance. We think we touched all the bases when we made our sales presentations but we may have only touched a nerve that started the prospect's association solid state module going in his computer, which led to his ultimate decision. The fastest computer in the world is the human brain. The limitations are that each brain can only store that which it has learned; and, secondly, it can not print out as fast as a screen or forward and backward as a printer. The mouth just won't work that fast.

Did you ever wonder why you wake up at 3:20 in the morning, look straight up at a dark, blank ceiling, can't fall back to sleep and think the clearest thoughts we ever had in our life? Do you wonder what made a particular past problem or a future planning situation come to your mind first thing on awakening at that goofy hour? There is a reason and I'll explain it, but first, I must comment that your thoughts at 3:20 am are correct. Rely on your naked, unfettered, unbiased, clearest thinking. Usually that early morning thought is the only one on your mind. Stand by your computer's midnight decisions; mark them down before you forget them. Then follow them to conclusion when print out time is at hand. You were right at 3:20 am to 3:50 am. Don't let your narrow tunnel vision and outside sources change your mind later.

After the sleep hiatus, you fall back to sleep and wake at the usual hour, generally not to think of the interruption again. Your wife may even tell you to stop these early morning "can't sleep" sessions because you're keeping her awake.

Now, for the reason that you wake up: professional head people call it your subconscious but I liken it to the computer lull after it's been shut off for the night and before it gets ready to go the next day. Your mind, through its subconscious, has just digested all the information from yesterday, every little piece of it, and is now in its purest rested state—getting ready for another day's programming.

I sell to this phenomenon, too. I tell businessmen that I would like to meet with them for the earliest appointment when they start their day. They ask, "What time, 8:00 or 8:30?" I say, "No! At 3:20 in the morning when you start your business day by looking straight up at the ceiling!" I generally get the response, "How did you know about that?" See, most businessmen are just like you. They lie awake at night, also. I tell them I'd like to do the appointment at 3:20 in the morning in their bedroom when we both have the most lucid minds. It works in getting me more meaningful attention during appointments. They keep thinking, "What else does this guy know about me? I better listen to him."

The point of all this is to associate the product with the need and the sale is easier. I know of salesmen who write on the policy contract "Mortgage Policy," "Billie's Education Policy," "Retirement Policy." I think that's great, that reaffirms the need. It puts it right with the solution. I once sold a retirement income policy by telling the client that I was there to give him a birthday present. It just so happened that the day of the interview was, in fact, his birthday. I told him I was going to give him $160 a month starting on July 11, 1998, which was his retirement birthdate. The income would start right on his birthday and would undoubtedly be the best gift anyone ever gave him. All he had to do was begin writing a check for $38 starting this day. He bought. The power of association was overwhelming. So spend only 90 seconds more before each appointment thinking about the need and with what you can associate it so that it makes a binding impression. You really get inside of a person's thinking when you can find the one real motivating force that he wants. He'll love you and your product and be a tremendous repeat buyer and center of influence.

7. The Shocking Game

Sometimes contrary to association, we have to be starkly honest rather than diplomatic. The blunt truth will shock and, anger, but win respect for your honesty and willingness to risk everything in one action. Some of the readers may object to this next little example but to be perfectly honest rather than diplomatic, let them write their own book and I'll buy a copy to read the rebuttals.

I had an appointment forthcoming with a wealthy client who was not very serious about his insurance or his estate planning. He bought insurance from me strictly as a defensive measure. He was also in a sales business and always liked to spar with me since he liked the sales ideas he picked up. He bought little policies and the reasons I stayed with him were that his family and mine were close and, secondly, there was a tremendous need which he could afford to cover. He earned well over $150,000 a year and had about $65,000 of insurance.

In the few days before the interview I found myself constantly thinking about his family. I liked Sally and the kids and I wanted them protected. I felt I had to do something to really startle him into being serious. The interview happened to be the day after Halloween. That evening, after the beggars had stopped coming to my door and my own kids were home on the floor counting and trading goodies, I was watching my daughters when I had a thought. I asked Dori if I could have the orange plastic bag she had just been using for tricking or treating. She gave it to me.

The next day I put Al's file in the Halloween bag and went to his office. His secretary made some joke about my being out begging and I laughed with her. When I got into Al's office he looked at the bag and didn't know what to expect so he said nothing about it. I laid it on his desk. We made small talk for a few minutes and finally he asked, "What's the bag for?"

I kept a stern look and said, "It's a briefcase for dummies and I have your file in it. The way things stand now Sally doesn't know what she's going to be left with when you die. The government and creditors will get treated and she'll get tricked. Can we now look at this problem seriously?"

He took just a few studious seconds and said, "Yes."

Another shocker which I have used sucessfully is to fill out a beneficiary form for existing client's policies as an interview. I start the appointment by saying, "Will you sign this form?" The answer is always a question, "What is it?"

I explain, "It's a beneficiary change form. The only cash you own is this small amount of life insurance. I've done the estate cost calculations and the government is going to get all of your insurance. I've made out the beneficiary form to the Government of the United States of America. That way, even though they get the money, we can save considerable administration costs by not having to have them wrench it away from your family."

It has worked very well for me.

8. The Down Payment Game

I believe that we all have to pay back something for the success we achieve. If you feel you haven't yet achieved the degree of success to make you secure, make a contribution and consider it a down payment. It will come back to you manyfold. Honest effort and honest intentions never go unrewarded. We all must get involved in our community so we pay back something of what we derive from it. If you haven't already signed up for all those fund raisings, committees, and religious organizations that no one else wants to do, do so right away. You will not be initiating an action. You will be paying back while at the same time making an investment. Somebody you have never even met has already made an investment for you. After all, we don't destroy a bridge just because we may never go that way again. If anything, we should improve on what has gone before and inertia will cause others to do the same, and the beat goes on. Getting involved and contributing time will not take any of your time at all. You will find that it gives you more time for the important things. I can't explain it. I don't know why. Just call it "new math." I can't explain that, either.

The philosphy is the same with study. As you invest more time in a progressive, worthwhile venture it forces you to become more productive in your daily chores. Everything becomes more intense and hones in on the most important aspects. I found as I studied for my CLU and then the advanced courses, I spent more time in study and supposedly less in work. My income continued to go up. New math, again.

I do some public speaking and I do some writing. But more important than any of that, I have found that one of the most important things I do is spend time helping other salesmen. I feel honored that they would call on me in time of strife, or indecision, or trouble. I admit it does take time but my philosophy is that I owe them because someone else previously spent time with me. I didn't get to this place in the universe alone. People have helped me in the past by sharing their storehouses of things I didn't have. Others have helped me by public speeches and writings they have made that have been copied by me entirely or have stimulated thoughts that have evolved into procedures that I use.

I finish every public speech with the same line. I tell this same thought to anyone who comes into my office for a free help session. "I have spent an hour with you and it was my pleasure, but I don't work for free so each of you owes me something and it isn't money. Each of you owes me an hour. Sometime when someone needs some handholding, some listening, some talking to, or just some company, you spend an hour with him. Then you will have paid me back. And tell him to pass it on and he will have paid you back."

9. The Fear-Deception Game

On occasion, we all know we have been lied to. A falsehood by any other name is still a lie. We hear them all the time: "The check's in the mail," "He's in a meeting," "Let me call you right back," "I didn't get your letter," etc. Once again, we are not all lily-white and I'm sure we have been the offenders at times. Most of these lies come as an avoidance method. We just don't want to face a person or face up to a situation. Sometimes we must remind ourselves that thinking about death or even growing old strikes a very real fear in some people.

I relate to you a situation which shows what I think is a real case of fear of both of the things for which we provide financial protection. I did estate planning for a forty-one year old man. In the first session, he told me that his father was a multi-millionaire. I told my client that it would be difficult to complete his planning accurately because we didn't know what the size of the inheritance was going to be or what the exact disposition of his father's estate would be. He had an older sister, his mother was deceased, and father had not remarried. With no marital deduction, the estate taxes would be huge. My client was involved in two businesses with his father and his only interest in the estate was getting the business interests. He had no idea of what his father's will said so he was very desirous of having the planning done which would allow him to stay in business, owning 100% on the father's death. He was willing to enter into buy-sell agreements or follow any equalization type distribution under the will but he did not want to be in business with his sister. Whenever he would discuss planning with his father, he was reassured that "it was taken care of." But he was not convinced and was very anxious.

I was quite willing to approach the father directly but the son felt it would be easier if the attorney, who represented both of them personally and in the corporations first mentioned the subject. I thought I had an excellent prospect but I had to place the case on the back burner. One day the son called me to say that his father had seen the lawyer and because of the lawyer's recommendation, he was now ready to meet with me. I was forewarned how tough the father was and coached on how to deal with him. I decided for myself that I would be forceful and direct and honest rather than diplomatic. I called the senior Mr. H. at 7:30 one morning. I introduced myself and he acknowledged that he knew my name by saying, "What an ungodly hour to call someone for business."

I responded with, "I always start my day at this time and your son said you'd be in at this hour." We arranged the appointment. I felt I was on a good basis after our phone conversation and I was looking forward to the meeting.

When I arrived for our 10 am appointment, the father was not there. His secretary said he had been in and my name was on his calendar but he must have forgotten and gone to the other business. She tried to get him by phone but to no avail. I had been stood up. She apologized and said he would call me. After a few days he hadn't so I called his office. The secretary said he was not in but he had mentioned he was going to call me. While this was going on the son was out of town on a vacation. When I talked to him on his return he was shocked in disbelief.

He had spoken with his dad that day and asked how we had gotten along. The father told him, "Burt's a nice guy; should we give him the pension?"

The son said, "That wasn't the purpose of the meeting. The pension is in good shape and Burt said it should stay where it is."

Father said, "That's OK, I'll be seeing him again." Why the father lied neither one of us can figure. Based on the background the son had given me, however, I can only surmise that fear is the reason. The case is very recent and as of this writing I still have not seen the father. I'm very anxious to do this interview because I'm sure he needs help and I can provide it by the use of our tools. I am bound to see him because of the fact I am in and out of their businesses. I am also confident that I will be able to do the planning for him. I feel confident that I will complete the insurance sale because the stalling routine did no good in the overall scheme of things. But more importantly, to my mind, he is now indebted to the son, lawyer and me to let the truth win out. He's been caught in his own deception and eventually he'll have to face reality. To do otherwise is financial suicide.

10. The Company Store Game

In the song *Sixteen Tons* there is a line which goes, "I owe my soul to the company store." The reference is to the early days of the coal mining industry when the miners worked long hours for little pay and in fact were indentured to the employer. The work was done on land owned by the company; the housing was owned by the company with rent being a part of the compensation package; and the sale of life's staples was offered only at the company store. There were no such things as shopping centers with wide assortments of goods. There was no need for it; there was no place to go where anything other than food and meager clothing was needed. As a result, the company store had the necessities of life and nothing else. Since the pay came from one source, money was almost obsolete. There was no need for it; in fact, it was just a nuisance; it messed up the bookkeeping to have another item called "dollars." All that was necessary was a method of keeping track of what the total purchases were. If a family exceeded its ability to pay, no real problem existed since the worker had no opportunity to go anywhere else. There wasn't even time to look. Credit was easily offered and gotten. The workers and families were kept as healthy as possible since they were absolutely necessary to the continuing function of the mining process just as a drone bee is absolutely necessary to the continuing function of a beehive. Coal or honey was the object and the worker had a limited and limiting function. So the worker was taken care of as long as he was useful. The tabs at the company store were like the debit accounts of the young insurance agent. Sometimes they mounted up but a little more was always available. Eventually, when the system was totally accepted by the employees, there was little else to do about it but talk, or as in many oppressive plights, sing. Therefore the line, "I owe my soul to the company store." This certainly was the place where unions were necessary.

However, in many situations where the worker has a choice he prefers the "company store" type of existence. Not to the point where "death do you part" is the goal but to the point of a certain degree of protectionism. This comes about through the phenomena known as fringe benefits. Some benefits are company offered and self-sustaining and some are purchased outside and require insurance. Sometimes in sales situations we, as salesmen, are frustrated by the attitude of "my group insurance will take care of me." I admit it is exasperating if you happen to be selling the individual benefits but it may not be so onerous if we were on the other end, as the agent selling the group benefit. So all of life is a balance. One man's benefit can be another man's overdose. Let's examine one case.

In 1957 I sold a $5,000 Life Paid-Up at 65 policy with a $25,000 decreasing term rider to a 25-year old man. The purpose of the rider was mortgage redemption. The total premium was under $200 annually and was a perfect package for a young family. The wife was delighted with all the benefits of this balanced program, especially the fact that she could keep her house when her husband died. She mentioned to me that her father was 56-years old and she came from a large family and had a two year old sister. She said this kind of policy would be perfect for her parents and asked if I would call on them. I told her I would be happy to if she could help me get the appointment. She called and I made the appointment with Mr. Small, the father.

When I got to the interview, he told me how tough he was and how he kept his section under control at the plant where he was foreman. He didn't have to be as explicit as he was since I spotted it right away. At that time in my career, I had not sold many people older than myself and I was a little out of my comfort zone just because of the age. Add to that the fact he was an obnoxious old guy and I didn't care whether I sold him or not, I just wanted to get out.

He asked me what the premium was for the same plan his daughter had bought and I showed him the illustration I had prepared in advance. He almost laughed as he told me how outrageous the premium was. He told me he had a full year's salary in a group benefit program and he paid nothing. He really had me intimidated and he started conducting the interview, not me. I pointed out that his $12,500 group benefit was term insurance and all the negatives of term. He sent me into my rate book to calculate the rate for $12,500 of 20 payment life, and this was the days before pocket calculators. He thought this premium was absolute thievery so I then figured the premium for whole life. This was no better to him and he asked me what else I had. He was really enjoying the interview and brought all conversation back to his group insurance. I told him all the conditions of group insurance, such as reduction of benefits at age 65, possible cancellation by the insurance company or his company. I told him his fringe benefits were only a condition of employment and could be changed for any number of reasons. His response came with a deep baritone proprietary voice; "Kid, the only way I'll ever lose my group insurance is if Hudson Motor Car Company goes out of business."

About a year later when Hudson had gone out of business, Mr. Small called me. During the interim a couple of things had happened: I had matured a little on the Linton scale but devastation had struck the Small family. When I met with him, he was not the same man I had previously seen. He was nervous, scared, timid, and generally a beaten man. I didn't like being pushed around on the first interview but I was young and could take it. But I also didn't like to see a change in an individual for all of the reasons he had to change. I liked him better the other way because now he was old and couldn't take it. He explained all of the trauma that occurs when someone loses a job and all of the frustrations that happen because no one wants a 57-year old foreman with 35 years of experience. In general, 1958 was a very poor financial year and he was degraded into having to beg for one or two days work in assorted tool and die shops that had work going.

He asked me what the premium was for $12,500 of insurance. I didn't have to ask if he meant term or permanent. I quoted the term premium and since he never in his life had paid any premiums, let alone the fact that there was now depression in his life, he was shocked by the figure. We set up $18,000 of decreasing term to cover his mortgage. The premium was about $15 a month and many times in the next few years he would slip into the grace period and sometimes beyond. On occasion I paid a premium for him and he paid me back. He died a few years ago and the claim was paid and the cash used for exactly the purpose intended, paying off the mortgage. Mrs. Small at least had her home to stay in although she had little else.

Group benefits are both a blessing and a curse. For those persons who would do nothing else, it's great. For those who use it as an excuse to ward off evil spirits such as insurance men trying to sell personal insurance, it's a detriment. For the agent selling to this market the spectre of group and association type of benefits can be a great source of consternation. For those who set up the plans for the employers, it can be a great source of income. As with all forms of competition, the choice of products in and of itself is the most positive aspect of growth possible. When a person has the choice to rely on group benefits or add to them, overall the population as a whole will come out better. It is far better to install all the group concepts and individual concepts rather than have more government-supplied benefits. When I used to hear the objection, "The Government will take care of me," I would respond with, "Yes, the same way it has taken care of the American Indian." I think, in the big picture, the widest possible choices of group or personal benefits typify the "law of supply and demand."

The real problem for the middle income earner is that group benefits can lull him to sleep with a false sense of security. There are so many uncertainties with the "company store" philosophy that an employee can find himself out in the cold with no protection for any number of uncontrollable reasons. We, as insurance salespeople, should try to protect this possible condemnation of our efforts. Many agents who sell company employee benefits do sell salary allotment and voluntary contribution type plans. They do attempt to coordinate the company plans with the employee personal program. Some companies are too big to attempt to meet individually with each employee. A good suggestion for this type of company would be for the successful large producer who sells the fringe benefits to make an alliance with one or more younger agents who have the time and desire to call on the employees on a single basis. This way all parties come out on the plus side; the company, the employee, the original producer, and the younger, smaller producer. This is a win-win-win-win situation. Some younger agents who might otherwise fail in the business could be helped to remain by using this "Big Brother" method.

Therefore, a caution to all of us: the group benefits we sell, including the jumbo kind, can either be an antitoxin or a poison. We can help or hurt ourselves and the public. As with all good things, moderation and restraint are necessary. Too much candy can taste bad.

11. The Fall Out of Your Chair Game

We've all heard the expression, "I fell off my chair." It's used to express surprise. I had a very funny situation where a client actually fell out of his chair. It doesn't express any particular pattern or moral as some of these other "games" do; but it is a humorous story that I like to tell.

The client is a very famous Detroit heart surgeon whose income is about $400,000 per year. He is incorporated and has a modest retirement plan with no life insurance in it. He owned only $100,000 of insurance; really small for the size of the income and the estate. An appointment was arranged by the doctor's attorney who went with me to the doctor's hospital office. The attorney's sense of urgency was dominant since he was proposing a defined benefit pension plan with a contribution about four times the size of the existing plan, along with a very sizable chunk devoted to insurance. The plan already had the endorsement of the C.P.A.

The attorney and I were kept waiting about twenty minutes in the private office but we were assured by the secretary that, "The doctor is just finishing up and will be leaving the O.R. in just a few minutes." I thought to myself that I couldn't participate in life and death type surgery and immediately go into a business meeting. I thought I would have been emotionally spent and couldn't make a decision on anything, but the attorney assured me this was the way he always talked to the surgeon and nothing was out of the ordinary routine on this day. Truthfully, I still felt I would have rather postponed the appointment and done it some other time. I was really apprehensive.

When the doctor came in, we were introduced by the lawyer and spent quite a few minutes with social talk before the lawyer brought us to business. I was fantastically impressed with this doctor's composure and ability to be calm after what I imagined to be a very tense operating room scenario. The lawyer then turned the meeting over to me and asked me to explain the workings of the plan. The doctor was relaxing and leaning back in his swivel chair. I had just mentioned the premium when there was a loud snap and the doctor disappeared behind his desk. His chair had broken. Both the lawyer and I quickly stood up and ran around the desk.

It was fortunate that it was a high-backed chair as the doctor had not hurt himself but was sure a lot less composed than he was a few moments before. In his disorientation, he rolled out of his chair, under his credenza and was on his hands and knees about to stand up when I quickly reached over to hold his head down so he wouldn't thump it. He thanked me as he crawled out from under the credenza.

It was only a funny coincidence but we should remember that sometimes a premium even twice the amount, let alone ten times the amount a client is presently paying, will knock him out of his seat. It truly was hilarious when it was all over to see this 60-year old sophisticated professional brought down to his hands and knees by the heavy blow of premiums.

12. The Ultimate Game

As a slang term I've heard people refer to someone else's business as a "game" or a "racket." I'm sure everyone has heard the phrase, "How is the insurance game?" So let's take off on this theme. Let's assume there was no bad intention in the using of this term and it was just one more American euphemism.

To the young man coming into the business, this ain't no game. To the hard-working serious agent, this ain't no game. To the wives and children of the agents on the firing line, this ain't no game. And most of all, to the policyowners and, ultimately the beneficiaries, this is most assuredly not a game. A game connotes fun but it has winners and it has losers. We have fun in our business but that's the spirit of enjoying what we're doing and we can certainly be winners or losers. Maybe that is why our business is so closely aligned with sports.

But I take serious offense to the thought that the insurance business is a racket. For sure, we've all heard this slander. Sometimes it comes from the most unobtrusive individuals. Everyone seems to think it's open season on insurance men. They say things in the most venomous tones that they wouldn't dare say to other businessmen, lest they find themselves involved in another game, namely boxing.

Let's talk about the winners. They are the clients, the beneficiaries, agents, companies, and in total, the whole economy. Therefore, if we're in a racket, I can't think of a better one in which we're all on the winning side. It's been going on commercially for over 250 years and the players must like it because the public, by the dominating law of supply and demand, is calling the signals.

9

If The Shoe Fits

When I hear this old cliché I mostly think of someone putting someone else in his proper place, but doing it in a safe fashion. If we use the safety of someone else's poetry which is anonymous, ancient and familiar, we can feel somewhat safe even if the phrase itself doesn't fit. The listener has to do some introspection to examine if the saying fits him and whether the speaker has the right to use it. The listener can't be too angry because he has to think of the rest of the thought himself. The person who says, "If the shoe fits, wear it," has only to utter these words and let the other party's mind run wherever it will in imagining what is meant. The quote is usually the end of a conversation and not meant to be a stimulant but, most frequently, a "put-down." I have heard the phrase said many, many times but I have never heard it said by a person who would be the most natural to use it, a shoe salesman.

One of the great parts of our job is fitting the right product to the right person for the right situation. We've already discussed term or permanent for the right situations; an annuity is not the right product for a mortgage need. Our choices of products are really not as wide as we think; after all, there are only a few types of policies, term, ordinary life, limited pay, endowment and annuities. Why then, do we have so much correspondence from home offices, brokerage managers, and outside sources, telling us they have the perfect answer for specific situations? Why is there so much change going on for something that is so static? In another vein, the whole purpose of pension plans is one thing:

retirement. However, think of all the imaginative variations there are in this field. When insurance is owned by a retirement trust, it boils down to a narrow selection of products; either term, permanent or annuities.

I once addressed a home office training class of young agents who were studying business insurance. Their school had lasted a week and they had discussed all forms of advanced underwriting. They had done studying, heard lectures, played roles with each other, videotaped their presentations, and used other modern machinery and devices to get a handle on the mysterious world of business insurance. I spoke on the last day of their school just prior to the time they would be breaking to go home. I was given a free choice on what my subject would be. I felt that after a week of book learning and "automatic" closes and "neat" sales after they said the words they had just studied, I had to make the message simple on how I achieved any success I had in the business market.

They had learned all the magic words such as "qualified," "deferred compensation," "integrated," "salary continuation," "key man," "irrevocable trust," "tax free loans," "medical-dental reimbursement," "target benefit," and the most alluring of all, "deductible." Their experience ranged from seven months to seven years but at this moment, after a full week of indoctrination, they were all "Top of the Table" members. It was my job to bring them back to reality while at the same time not discouraging them. All the time I knew that the lawyers, accountants, bankers, comptrollers, shareholders, and other assorted advisors were waiting for them to come back next week to see whose schooling was better. They compare notes and go to school, too, you know. I decided to try and condense the message down to one word. For instance, a policy in a word is a contract; a train is a vehicle consisting of passenger cars, freight cars, engine, running on a track, etc. I had to get this one word firmly fixed in their minds so they understood the big picture. It was a situation of "all roads lead to Rome," and "there's no way to get there from here" at the same time. The word I chose was "application."

I asked if anyone had ever sold any retirement policies with this company. There were a few "Yes" answers. I asked the color of the policy. Answer--green. I asked what type of insurance. Answer--permanent.

I asked if anyone ever sold any deferred compensation. There were a few "Yes" answers. There was also one guy who said everytime he missed on a sale he thought his compensation was deferred. I asked the color of the policy. Answer--green. I asked what type of insurance. Answer--permanent.

I asked the same questions for split dollar, key man, and buy–sell insurance. I got the same answers--green, permanent policies. We, therefore, reasoned together that if all the policies came out of the same underwriting department and were the same color and the same type, there were no differences in the policies themselves. The difference was in the application of the purpose of those policies. It solved some of the bewilderment of the advanced sale area and we went on to a very fine dialogue about the ''needs'' selling of business insurance. Even in the big leagues we have come back to exposing the problem and to using colored paper to solve it. Our job is making sure the shoe fits.

I had a situation where the shoe fit the situation perfectly but the feet started to go in different directions. I was subpoenaed to appear at a court hearing between two clients who were supposedly equal shareholders in a chain of car parts stores. At issue was the percentage of the business owned by the respective parties. I brought all my files with me into court. Apparently my testimony was important because the proportions of insurance in force per store would prove who owned what. The trial was messy but I thought one lawyer was on the right track by making a case on this basis. Of course, a buy-sell agreement, corresponding with proper documentation on the stock certificates, would have done a better job but the crux of the problem was that this proof was not available because it had never been done.

At that time I was doing my filing in three-ring loose-leaf binders. I had a number of books because of the number of stores. When I was on the witness stand I would refer to the books to answer questions about dates and amounts and other information. One of the attorney's asked me if he could see the books. I told him ''No.'' He was upset and appealed to the judge. The judge asked my why I wouldn't show him the books and I answered that I had not been instructed by the bench. The judge said the two words that allowed me to be neutral and maintain a working relationship with both sides after the trial; ''So instructed.'' He took the monkey off my back.

I gave the attorney the binders and the judge called a recess. After about a half-hour the judge recalled the court to order. I took the stand and was reminded I was still under oath. The attorney handed the books back to me and asked only a few more questions. The last few, I thought, were off his subject. He asked, with emphasis, "Are **all** these books your records for just this one business?"

I answered, "Yes."

He said, "It looks to me like you've made a lot of money on these two clients."

I said, "Yes, but from the looks of it, not as much as you're going to make." This was a classic case of "If The Shoe Fits." He was mad but could only get back as good as he tried to give. He could only say, "No more questions."

For diversion let's forget about the shoe fitting and switch to a story about the hair fitting. I made a sale of stock redemption insurance to a corporation with two equal shareholders. One policy came to me standard and the other had a three dollar per thousand rating. This wasn't a typical rating where the businessman had sacrificed his health for his wealth; I thought it was justified. The client was 6′ 5″ tall and weighed 285 pounds. When I came for the delivery, he was very upset with the extra premium and said he would not take the policy. I pointed out this would defeat the proposed buy-sell agreement but he said it was all right with him if Jerry took his policy but as for himself he was going to diet for six months, get to 225 pounds and then call me. I told him I was not concerned with "diet" but "die." He was resolute so we placed the one policy as a keyman policy without having a stock redemption agreement drawn.

Just about six months later, Dale called me and said he was ready to get re-examined. The policy was issued as standard and his weight was listed as 225 pounds. When I saw him on the policy delivery, he was beautiful. He was truly slim, his new clothes were sharp and he had bought himself a toupee. I complimented him on losing 60 pounds and he corrected me saying he had lost 100 pounds. It seems he had not stepped on the scale for the first exam, just told the doctor what he weighed. Why the doctor accepted the oral statement I don't know but what's 40 pounds between friends at that weight?

We completed our business whereupon he looked at my bald head and said, "Burt, I want to buy you a hairpiece."

I responded, "No thanks."

"But you helped me out. The guy who made this is in Dearborn. He does the best work."

"How did I help you, Dale?"

"You're the only guy who ever got me mad enough to really lose weight. It's only $400. I want to make you a gift."

I said, "Dale, you aren't making much sense. You wouldn't pay $600 for a justifiable health reason but you want to buy me a gift hairpiece for $400?" That's how it stood. I never took the hairpiece; he took the insurance. Happily, he has not put the weight back on. The moral of this story is about as explainable as why there is a taboo on wearing white shoes before Memorial Day and after Labor Day but "if the shoe fits. . .

The shoe fitting is one case but when it never wears out that's another. In 1968 a casualty agent came to me and said he had a prospect for a retirement plan but didn't know the field; could we work on a joint basis? The propsect was a small city just outside of Grand Rapids. We met with Ken, the city manager, who flatly refused to give us the census information. He explained that he was asked by the city council to get proposals from ten sources and he had just cut it off at twenty-five. It seems that everyone had a friend or relative who was selling retirement plans and wanted to put in a bid. I admit the odds seemed long but the smell of a challenge started to excite me. Bob prevailed on Ken to let us have a census list and cutoff the bids after that. Ken relented.

When we got to my office to look at the list we saw the plan was to be a six percent defined contribution plan with normal retirement age at 65. That's all it told us besides the fact the city would pay three percent and the employee would match it with three percent. Remember, this was 1968. The salaries were in the $6,000 to $13,000 range and because it was a small town, most of the employees had long seniority and a rather high average age. After we calculated a few pensions we saw that they were going to be minimal. I quickly determined this was no place for speculation, only guarantees. There would be no room for split-funding. If ever there was a need for fixed annuities, there it was, right on this census list.

Bob didn't know if he agreed with me but he also didn't understand pensions. We also determined, since there was no other fringe benefit other than a medical plan, we should recommend a flat $2,000 group life plan to start after thirty days employment. We finished our cost and benefit sheet and went to see the city manager. There I saw the most amazing sight I had ever seen in my life. Ken's office was massive; the building seemed like it was not originally a city hall but converted from a plant. Over in one corner he had his desk and credenza; he also had room for a ten-person conference table, two 4′x5′ tables filled with plans and documents, and a drafting board. His background was engineering and he had the usual pocketful of pens, protractors, rulers, notebooks, and blue ink spots. On the walls were easel sheets, typed with each of the twenty-six vendors listed. The sheets were lined-off with columns such as investment yields, loan interest rates, business in force, assets, dividend history, etc. There was a color code with green being the best. I saw our company listed and we had a couple of green marks and other colors, too. He was proud of his work. To my mind this was the original consultant. Any insurance company would have been willing to pay him a $75,000 consulting fee just for the imagination and showmanship.

I asked him what it represented and he told me that he found it very interesting to examine all of the facets of the various bidders. Besides, he thought he should be prepared to assist the city council when the time came. I asked him where he had gotten all of this information. He responded, "From this" and with the alacrity of a swordsman going into action he held up a Flitcraft. He loved that book and told me he found it fascinating reading. Apparently, someone who thought his proposal was the best gave it to him. The companies represented on the walls were insurance companies, mutual funds, stock brokerage houses and two banks. The plans ranged from mutual funds to split funded insurance plans.

When we showed him our spread sheet, he said it was the worst. Our figures were the lowest of all twenty-six entities. I explained our philosophy of "guarantees" to him and the fear that a 56-year old man who was only going to have a $110 monthly pension might lose ten percent at the risk of making ten percent. He wasn't convinced since 1968 was the boom times for the mutual funds and their figures were very high. He told us that it was his job to eliminate all but seven companies, each of whom were to make a twenty minute presentation to the council. He said he was going to give us a chance to make a presentation just so the council could see the "most conservative approach."

On the appointed day, we made our presentation in front of the council and mayor. The citizen was out in force: one. (No misprint! One citizen, or maybe a city worker, had shown up.) We used an easel along with agendas for the members. Our theme was one word: "Guarantees.'' The next day Ken called us and said he still didn't understand why, but we were the company chosen to install the pension plan.

In November of 1969, we asked for the new census information and Ken said we ought to review the plan with the council. We showed up for the meeting a few minutes before the 10 am starting time. The mayor, who also owned a gas station, came sliding in five minutes late while asking, ''Burt, how long is your part going to take?''

I said, ''Two minutes if the one question I know will come up is asked, otherwise forty-five seconds.''

He mumbled something about slick salesmen and said, ''Let's get started.''

I asked them to turn in their minute book of the previous year to the date on which we had our meeting. Since it was a municipality it seemed the paper shuffling in finding the right sheet was in order. When they all finally had the right sheet I said, ''Please look at the sheet, we're right on target.'' And I shut up.

One of the council members said, ''How much money did we lose?''

I said to the mayor, ''That's the question.'' I answered, ''Nothing. If you remember my presentation of last year and if you will look at the column that is entitled 'Guaranteed Income' you'll remember that my whole presentation was based on guarantees.''

''But Burt, you know the mutual funds and the market have turned. We lost on the sidewalk fund, the building fund, and others. Didn't we lose anything on the pension?''

''No, all the figures are guaranteed. I don't know what the value is today because I haven't calculated it, but you haven't lost a penny and you're right on schedule.''

''You sure?''

''Yes.''

''What do you need?''

''I'll see Mary, the city clerk for information on new employees, terminated employees, new salaries, and a check.''

''OK, thanks. Next order of business?''

That shoe definitely fit and still does.

Another way that our product fits is that it stands alone on it's own merit and if presented for what it represents it doesn't need any other side deals. We need not fear that honesty and fair bargaining will hurt or destroy a deal. I'll give you an example with a very humorous story.

I have a client who owns a medium sized manufacturing business. He got his corporate training working for one of the very large international companies for ten years, from age twenty-one to age thrity-one. He started as a salesman and ended up as a very high ranking vice-president. Along the way he had made about ten moves from city to city. He gave up the large corporate life because he didn't like the skullduggery and constant intrigue between the ladder-climbers and schemers. The result of this was a very efficient, calculating, shrewd executive.

He started work promptly at 9 am each day and left precisely at 5 pm. He took a full one-hour lunch promptly at noon each day. He only allowed two minute appointments to his employees and fifteen minute appointments to anyone else. He felt these decisions should only be made after the course of action had been carefully planned.

I called him just about age-change time to discuss conversion of a large block of term insurance. He explained to me that his auditors were in and he had to stay in the office for lunch for the next few days. He wondered if I could see him in his office during that time. He said he would have a sandwich for me. I told him that was fine since I was only going to have an orange for lunch. He said the orange sounded good so I said we would have a sandwich and an orange for lunch. I arrived about twenty minutes early for the appointment. When his secretary announced me he asked if I could come right in.

When I got in his office we exchanged about thirty seconds of, "How's Sharon?" "How's Elaine?" I then opened my briefcase and put two oranges on his desk. We completed the paperwork for the conversion in quick order. He explained that his schedule was way off because of the audit. He said, "I let you in early, can I kick you out early?"

I replied, "No problem," and grabbed the two oranges and put them in my case.

He said, "That's my orange."

"No, it's not."

"You said you would give me an orange."

"You said you would give me a sandwich."

"Yes, but I didn't get time to get them."

"That's alright, you eat two sandwiches. I'll eat two oranges."

"You're kidding! Give me my orange."

"I'm not kidding."

"But I just bought insurance from you."

"What's that got to do with lunch?"

"C'mon, Burt."

"Nope." I moved toward the door. He came around the desk and stood against the door and said, "You're kidding, gimme the orange."

I said, "No," and opened the door.

Harold, his comptroller, was just walking by and said "Hi" to me and I said "Hello" to him.

Paul said to Harold, "He won't give me the orange." Now, realize there is no orange in sight. I have them both in my case.

Harold asked, "What are you guys talking about?"

Paul said, "I just bought a big policy and he said he would give me an orange."

Harold just smiled and said, "I gotta go. Give him the orange, Burt." I didn't give him the orange and left the office. A year later at age-change time, I spoke to him on the phone and he agreed to new coverage right away. I told him I would arrange the medical and meet him at the examiner's office to fill out the forms.

I arrived at the office about the same time Paul did. The EKG and X-ray were to be done in a lab one floor below the doctor's office so we went down there first. I had him sign the application and we both picked up magazines to read. As soon as he was engrossed, I opened my case and took out two oranges and put them on the table between us. He didn't look up from the book but shifted his eyes sideways to see the oranges. Suddenly, he snapped his left arm out and speared one of the oranges and started to peel it quickly. The lady sitting across from us must have thought our upcoming X-rays were for head problems. In fact, she tried to keep her mind on her book even though the action going on across from her was enticing. I took my orange, peeled it, and ate it. Not a word was spoken but I know he felt the score was now even and truthfully so did I. We didn't need words. The shoe fit.

I'll give you one more example of where the truth and, therefore, the shoe fit. I saw two equal shareholders in a lumber business who just appeared too eager to learn from me. They were paying attention so hard that I got the feeling they were cramming for an exam. Suddenly, I realized that was exactly what they were doing. They had told me early in the meeting about their strong church affiliation.

I felt something was wrong so I stood up and said, "I don't feel we're making progress here; I better go." They protested and asked what was the matter. I told them I felt they were pumping me for information to give to another insurance man, maybe a church brother. They looked like little kids with their hands in the cookie jar. Ashamed, they admitted I was exactly right. But they didn't want me to go. They wanted me to handle their business insurance but they felt obligated to the church brother who had approached them.

I said, "Deal with him, then."

They responded, "He doesn't know the business."

I suggested that if he didn't know the field, maybe he really didn't want to do it. I suggested they each call him and buy a $25,000 policy. I thought he would be happy with a $50,000 sale and I would handle the much larger and complex corporate case. They thought this was an excellent solution and agreed.

As it turned out, the other agent was delighted with the $50,000 sale. The clients were happy with my planning as was their attorney. I was happy to clear the air and get the larger sale.

The shoe fit for all parties. Especially so when one of them died in a car crash right in front of the lumber yard. This happened only seven months after the sales. He left four children at home. As always when we pay a claim I was very sad but the ambivalence came in because I had completed good financial planning for the corporation and the heirs.

10

Mecca

The Holy City. The desired place. The epitome. The best. The most. The place where only good things happen. The place where righteous, religious people yearn to go. The ultimate. Only good things can be generated by Mecca. We have our equivalent of Mecca in the insurance business.

We call it the Home Office.

This chapter will be a tongue-in-cheek exposé of the feelings of some field agents toward the Home Office, the feelings of some Home Office personnel toward the field, and my impression of what the symbiosis is and what it should be. I'm reminded of the old saying: "Each person is three people; one is what he thinks he is, secondly, what other people think he is, and thirdly, what he actually is." I mention all this by way of saying that this chapter is not meant to contain venomous intent toward either side but only to take a lighthearted look at both sides of the mailman's route.

I remember when I was in the military service and we were in ranks being lectured by our superior officers. We were required to stand at attention while the diatribe dragged on and on. The admonitions were extremely vitriolic. I couldn't believe that everything being said was really meant for us. We couldn't be as bad as we were being told. Two thoughts ran through my mind as I stood at attention, eyes forward, seeing but not looking. First, I thought, "This must be some kind of character-building regimen,'' and secondly, ''They're not talking to me, they're talking to the guy next to me.''

My instructions to each of you as you read this chapter is that it will build character and it isn't pointed at anyone in particular. Please take a healthy attitude of being able to laugh at ourselves and have some fun if you recognize some of these incidents.

AGENT'S NARROW-SIGHTED VIEW OF THE HOME OFFICE

When we first come into the business the mere mention of the words, ''Home Office,'' brings a feeling of blessed finality from which there is no question that everything is on the path to truth and righteousness. The managers, general agents, supervisors, trainers, and other recruiters hold the sacred place out to be the giver of all good things and the solution of all insoluble problems. The rookie hears about the training facilities at the Home Office and he uses the training material provided by it. There is no appeal higher than the ''Supreme Court'' somewhere out there. And the farther away the agency office is from the Home Office, the more sacrosanct are the proclamations. Sometimes we have questions from clients regarding why we must do certain things in certain ways regarding our insurance procedures. When we tell them, ''It's the law,'' there is usually no further comment and we move forward from this ''given'' fact. The same is true when the teacher mentions to the rookie that the facts at hand are those sent from the Home Office. All thinking stops at that point and anything to be added to the process comes over and above these unquestionable truths.

The rookie stays in awe of this place somewhere off in the blue yonder. He is shown beautiful pictures or postcards of the building itself. He places that in his memory bank of beautiful places right next to The Mint, The Capitol Building, Freedom Hall, The Colliseum, and The Pearly Gates. The pictures are always first rate, sometimes even being aerial shots from different angles showing the rest of the beautiful financial centers or office complexes in the background. As the freshman agent looks at this picture and is constantly hearing the magic phrase, ''The Home Office,'' he dreams of the day he can see it for himself. He hears offhand conversations about the Home Office from other agents or the office staff. He sees the complete reverence and acceptance of the gospel according to long distance or airmail. Sometimes he may have even been treated to a trip to the place during the courtship period.

He marvels at the open checkbook policy when he's told he doesn't have to spend a penny on this sojurn to Mecca. There are people who want to meet him and he sure wants to meet them.

Most times the novice doesn't get to the Home Office right away. This usually comes after a period of training and "experience" in the agency. This is also a grace period for the agent because any mistakes he makes or sales missed because he couldn't handle the situation will be corrected when he gets it in the hands of the experts at the Home Office. It always happens that a class had just finished the week before the agent signed a contract or the one starting two months from now will be too soon for the new man so the manager, in his wisdom, will hold the agent out until "the class will mean more to you." The agent builds his visions of sugarplum fairies and golden edicts because of the delay until the class is formed. In this class there will be agents from all over the country, all bringing the accumulated expertise of their agencies and wisened managers. And always there is one of them who just closed a one-million dollar case on the head of a *Fortune* 500 company after only twenty-nine days in the business.

Finally, the day is set. The manager coaches his agent because they both want to look good in front of the gurus at the Home Office. The agent is now representing mother, country, flag, apple pie, the local agency, and color TV. He is instructed on what clothes to bring, how much money to advance, what the curriculum will be and what dinners and Home Office functions there will be, on the night there isn't homework, of course. It's an exciting time and to top it off the freshman sees the TV commercial from one of the competitors where all the guys are in a classroom with their sleeves rolled up, desks full of papers and books, all the modern learning equipment, and everyone paying attention. Boy, he can hardly wait. Now when he misses a sale he says to himself, "No matter, I'm going to the Home Office. They'll show me what I did wrong. I'll never miss this kind of a case again."

His wife is anxious for him. She asks if she is invited, too. He explains with executive-like conciseness, "No, this is all work. You wouldn't enjoy it, anyway. I wouldn't have any time for you. But, Mr. Brown (he is still calling the manager Mister) told me today that next year's sales conference is going to be at the Muirberg, or the Greenberg, or the Greenbriar, or something like that. We'll have two days and a breakfast if I make it or five days and breakfast and lunch if I make the President's Top Gunners Club. Don't worry, Hon, I'll make the top club after I finish this course at the Home Office. And we're going on a plane, too."

Sometimes, there comes a little slump before the first pilgrimage to the Home Office and our salesman gets worried that maybe he'll be uninvited. So he presses a little harder. He may be having some mental pressures but the material keeps coming, including a plane reservation. Most times this is the true business Mt. Everest itself. He's never been on a plane before so he must be succeeding in the insurance business. He tells his friends, who are no longer just pals but they're now prospects, that he's going on a plane to the Home Office. He verifies his few clients' judgment by telling them that all's well on the Western Front or the East Coast, depending on what company. The manager continues coaching him, role playing, rehearsing sales talks, and keeps reminding him that "just because it's a corporation, that doesn't make it deductible, but they'll explain that to you next week."

That first trip is always exciting and the people are so nice and so intelligent. The agent wonders just exactly how much insurance these instructors sold to get to such a high position as "Associate for Advanced Underwriting Training Educator of Field Operations and Assistant Actuarial Vice-President for Computer Retaliation, Central Division." Besides that, they never take off their suit coats at the Home Office. He vows that he is going to get rid of this sport coat when he gets home and buy only suits.

The training is great and every simulated situation ends the same way—the prospect says the key word and you look down the plastic card for the right answer to the objection and another sale is made. The instructor says "great" and the class applauds, even the guy who said he sold 700 TSA's just the month before leaving home and wasn't sure if he really should have taken the trip. The teachers verify what the manager said in that they would be sending report cards back to the agencies, yet this is one of the best classes ever to be in the Home Office since the company last raised the dividend schedule. The class is teased with a little bit of advance information; "It's not official yet, we need final approval, but we expect a big announcement regarding dividends within a few days. Your managers will get the material soon but don't say anything to your clients." Our man calls his wife and the agency and his $30,000 policyholder and lets them know what a professional he's becoming. These are truly the best of times.

Along with the school there is an afternoon of tours to the various departments; the computer room, the mail room, the vault, and the museum showing the first policy ever issued and the desk with the pigeonholes used by the first president. On the last day of the school, one of the big producers of the company flies in and addresses the class on the importance of CLU, MDRT, NQA, and how his Home Office will help him attain it. The president of the company, ("Call me by my first name, Arthur") talks informally without any notes and the first impression of the Home Office is even more than anyone could have imagined. You part with the words ringing in your ear, "We're always here to help you. Just call."

Our rookie starts to produce, acquires some policyholders and needs service so he now starts looking for all the help the Home Office promised him. He calls a department head who bought him a drink and promised good service. The secretary said he was visiting agencies and would only be back in the office next Wednesday but he's got a full desk of reports and memos to do before he leaves the next day for the LIMRA meeting and then for his four week vacation. Could someone else help? "Yes, his assistant."

Response, "She's at a meeting; she should have been back by now. I can have her call you or possibly you could write a memo. It's really the best way."

So we now come to one of the most important functions of the Home Office and, incidentally, the paper industry; The Forty-One Memo syndrome.

From our high school physics classes we remember the boiling point of water, 212 degrees F. At 211 degrees, water is just hot. It will burn you, it will clean efficiently, and it makes great coffee but it doesn't boil at 211 degrees. Just the one extra degree trips the balance enough to make water boil. And when it boils it causes steam. And the steam can move huge tonnage ships, it can turn turbines and cause energy, it can harm you; the power is awesome. One little tiny degree makes all that difference.

In the usual scheme of The Forty-One Memo syndrome, the forty-first memo is like the two-hundred and twelfth degree; it does wonders. But nothing happens until the forty-first memo. It may say the very thing that the first one said but there is no thought or authenticity to a first memo. For sure, the first memo is worthless if it came from an agent. The last memo may very well say the same thing that the first one did but at least it came from a staff officer who knows what the public needs. After all, he has two parts of LUTC and he went to a seminar last week. I know of one true situation where two department heads sat about one hundred feet from each other. One called with a request for some material. The other said, "Send me a memo." So the man dictated a memo; his secretary typed it; put it in her *Out* box; it got delivered to the other secretary's *In* box; she took it to her boss; he studied it for four days; dictated a memo back saying he'd have to research the subject; it went in her *Out* box; got delivered the other way; this secretary gave it to her boss; who put it in his "To Do" pile. A round trip of two weeks took place—without result. About two weeks after this the first man was in the second man's office when he spotted the book he wanted on the shelf. He asked if he could take it. The second department head said, "I didn't realize that's what you wanted; write me a memo so I'll know who has it." So if you become frustrated sometime because of the slowness of a request, just ask what memo they're on. Occassionally, I lie and say I wrote three memos already when I really didn't, just trying to speed up the process to get to forty-one.

Sometimes disaster strikes when two phenomena occur at the same time and that is if one of the forty-one memos mention a consultant. For now let's assume we're by The Forty-One Memo syndrome and let's concentrate on the consultant, also known in Hollywood as the "stand-in." Insurance companies love consultants and vice-versa. If it was a real romance, they would go around carving each other's inititals in hearts on trees. Governments like consultants, too. The thicker his report and the more memos that have to be written to get it away from him, six months late, the more importance can be placed on it. Sometimes, it's like an agent writing a letter to get an appointment when both time and money can be saved by just picking up the phone.

Think of the safety in hiring a consultant to make a report for you. First off, the more he charges, the better he must be. When the report comes, the more paper included the better it must be. If the plan of action is used and is successful, the officer who hired the consultant takes the credit. If it's a bad plan, the consultant is blamed and the officer can keep the same seat in the officer's dining room. From the viewpoint of some Home Office people the Lord made heaven and earth in six days and on the seventh He rested, and on the eighth He made consultants.

Now, I realize that some of these comments, although written with a smile on my face, may appear slanderous to some Home Office types.

But, who among us have not heard the Home Office plaint, "This would be a good place to work if we didn't have agents." I don't fully understand the workings of the corporate ladder but I know they all read the same handbooks and keep them on their shelves or lower right desk drawers. Books such as *Winning by Intimidation, Up the Corporate Ladder, Power by Awareness, How to Get an Office With a Carpet, Without Leaving Your Desk, How to Get Your Name Moved Higher on the Inter-Office Memo List, Dress to Win, I Gave at the Office,* or *We Don't Socialize After Work,* and others such as, *Getting The Window Office with the Best Sunlight.*

I sometimes get the feeling that some Home Office people could be moved, blindfolded, to another company's Home Office, maybe across the country, maybe to another industry, and still function without losing a stroke. The first questions would be, "What cities are doing the best?" "How much of an increase do we project for the year?" and "Let's up the percentage by fifteen points." This last number is safe, by the way, because it's out of the single figure range yet doesn't appear too greedy.

Home Office people are away from their desks a lot of the time. Always for good reasons: blood bank, library committee, charities, meetings, special meetings, meetings to arrange future meetings, meetings to discuss cutting down on meeting time, special projects, or the catch-all, "He should be back any minute."

I once sat at a luncheon table with five officers of a major Home Office. One of them had just returned from a trip to his territory. He stayed at a hotel where they would not honor his travelers discount card. The hotel had the name of another officer of the same company, same address, but different division, but they wouldn't take this card. There was a lengthy discussion of how this should be handled. One of the junior officers said maybe it would suffice if a letter was written explaining that all holders of the card from this Home Office should be welcomed. Or secondly, a letter should be written asking for a blanket commercial discount for this company. He was told by his superior that he had a good idea. I thought it was a good idea and thought the subject was closed. But the ranking officer continued, "Bill, talk to Mark and get this subject on our management planning committee meeting agenda for the first possible time." What was going on here was a little bit of Forty-One Memo action to manipulate the idea around so the top man got the credit for the ultimate decision.

Actuaries—I love them and I won't make any jokes about them. I truly respect them because the numbers they give us really work. I take their word for it when they establish a rate. I would have no way of verifying their work except for the fact that the companies have always paid death claims and given loans when requested. But they are a breed unto themselves and I'm sure they say the same things about agents. They always seem suspicious of me when I say, "Hello" as if they were trying to figure out the hidden meaning. I really don't think they know what the agent does in the insurance scheme. Take this as a humorous little example. I don't know if it's typical but I heard it with my own ears.

I sat in on an agency-management advisory committee meeting a few years ago. It was a full-blown meeting with officers and department heads on the various subjects being discussed, all there. We were deeply involved in a discussion of certain plans and rates when an assistant actuary leaned over to his vice-president and whispered, "Do the agents have rate books?" At that moment I though that, although the oddsmakers in Las Vegas didn't have F. S. A. behind their name, they could do a better job than this clutz sitting at the conference table with us.

The most mystical part of the Home Office to me is the Underwriting Department, also referred to as The Dartboard. The bulls-eye seems small on some occasions, although I must admit it is on very few applications. The underwriting has truly been liberalized in the past few years. The mystery comes in because certain cases get extra premiums while others don't, even though the same circumstances seem to prevail. It is the ones that come out amended which is surprising to me, not the fact that a certain small percentage will not be prime rate. Another Ouija board pheonomenon is that brokerage managers always say their underwriting is the most liberal. This occurs sometimes between agents of two companies dealing with different people in the same company. Also, some of the risks that are reinsured by certain companies seem to be accepted when on other occasions, when this company is the prime carrier, the verdict is different. However, the biggest gripe with underwriting departments that I have seen is the need for "additional information." These extra trips are a nuisance, but more aggravating is the piggybacking of APP's and forms. Just when one is completed, here comes a request for another from another doctor or the request for "just one more form to be signed."

Speaking of forms to be signed, will the proliferation of forms ever stop? They keep coming. Frequently, they say nothing more than their forerunner. Sometimes we get notices that certain forms, because of their complexity, are being changed and simplified. This has not yet proven to be true at all. The imagination of some of our Home Office colleagues in designing forms is amazing. Each time they design a form it causes a ripple effect so that another department has to amend their forms to correspond. I've also had memos asking for forms that agencies didn't even have distributed to them. I once had some silly correspondence going regarding a beneficiary change. I couldn't get rid of the papers. They kept coming back for minor language changes or special designations made-up by the title department. I wondered what would happen if two agents around the country were changing beneficiaries at the same time. It appeared that mine was the most important event that had occurred since the introduction of the Guaranteed Insurability Rider. Finally, in exasperation, my secretary brought in a request from the Home Office for completion on a new form. I wrote a letter saying that we couldn't honor their most recent memo because they had not completed my office form B178. As you suspect, there was no such thing as a form B178, but the Home Office took it seriously and wrote me a memo saying they were sorry they couldn't locate B178 and would I send them a copy.

Some forms are redundant in some respects and shortsighted in others. I noticed this on the most important forms we have, part one. Look at yours just for fun. The "signature of applicant" line was half as big as the space provided for the date.

We need the Home Offices and they need us. I don't think anything is going to change in the future to bring us any closer. It hasn't in the past and with the diverse interests going on, I don't think it will in the future. We're locked in with each other and from this chaos comes order so let's go forward. But, like paddling a canoe, you pull a little to the left and a little to the right and in this fashion you go forward.

HOME OFFICE NARROW-SIGHTED VIEW OF THE FIELD: MERCENARY OR MISSIONARY?

The last segment was rough language, aimed at Home Offices. From what I've heard from salesmen of other products, their impressions of their Home Offices are the same. I look at some of these salesmen and at some of my colleagues and myself and I ask, "Are these guys always sweetness and light in their dealings the other way?" The answers will obviously indicate that there are two sides to any story. So let's zoom in on the agent under the microscope of the Home Office.

When the manager makes his recruiting report to the Home Office, or calls them, or writes to them, he bubbles with enthusiasm each time he hires a rookie. He gushes to his regional superintendant that, "This kid has more poise than anyone else I've ever seen. He played four sports at the local high school, played in the Potato Chip Bowl in Swingback, Michigan, picked up his own fumble in the end zone for the winning touchdown, and had all the pro basketball teams after him, but he was too tall. He married the most popular girl in the college graduating class and they're a well-liked, well-connected couple. You'll love him when you get to meet him. We got a winner here and he only needs $300 more than our maximum financing schedule, so get it approved for me, will you?" At this point, the agency supervisor thinks to himself, "Here goes old Denny again. Where does he get all of these winners?"

So the supervisor does what he can and gets the kid hired at a few bucks over. The manager goes into the intensive training routine, showing Special Agent X-9 all the basic material and even the secret stuff like his own W-2. At the Home Office, they're wondering why it is that the manager can't ever hire anyone within the new-man financing budget. But somewhere in the crowd a good one is going to come along someday so they back the manager's judgement and try again. Therefore, from the first contact the Home Office is placed in the position of blind faith with their men in the territory.

I already mentioned the viewpoint of the field toward the never-ending paper chase that goes on, but let's examine it from the Home Office side. As agents we must begin to appreciate the fact there is a central place where the records are kept as complete as possible. This includes getting adequate and complete information to the underwriter so a fair decision can be made both for the new applicant and the existing clients who already have been promised the conditions of their money for future delivery. If a mistake is made because of incomplete information, the payors will be the existing policyholders in the form of lower dividends in the future. Like anything else in life, the consumer ultimately pays for everything. I admire the underwriters for their objective attitudes, basing their decisions on a completely clinical paper picture of the applicant. True, most cases fall into fairly standard molds requiring no value judgments, but those that necessitate deep insight have to be weighed by the best professionals available, and that is not the biased salesman. That is a person charged with the responsibility of protecting and improving the system, and sometimes it requires more paper. Consider, sometimes it's you who has to do the chasing, but what if all questionable requirements were waived? For those of us doing the fullest supplying of information in the first instance, it won't make any difference . . . for a while. But then the slipshod applications of the marginal cases would result in earlier claims and ultimately higher net costs. In addition, the bad cases would proliferate. As an example, let's suppose one company was known to have particularly loose underwriting. Is it not logical to assume that every questionable piece of business would be submitted to this insurer? Is it not logical to assume also, that eventually this company would have a worse claim ratio than a more careful company? Is it not also logical to expect that if the practice were not checked early, that company would eventually be out of business? I think we would all prefer a good check-and-balance system. Therefore, we need good neutral decision makers. We may disagree with them sometimes but the underwriting corps is the best system we've got for evaluating applicants. So I can see the frustration of the underwriter when a plea comes with questionable cases for special consideration. I agree with them that the check and balance system is best left in their hands. I, for one, trust them more than I trust my fellow salesmen. Yes, and sometimes this means another request for paper.

I had one case where the underwriter made the right decision which required one more request form and resulted in a slightly smaller sale for me but ultimately helped me sell a lot more business. The applicant was me. In 1964, I had a kidney removed. When I got out of the hospital I was told that I would be uninsurable for five years and then rated $5 per thousand for two more years. I decided to convert some of the decreasing term I had as a rider on one policy. I calculated the amount at approximately $30,000 and sent in the conversion form for this amount. In the usual course of time I got the policy back for $29,647, along with an amendment form to sign for this proper figure. What this meant is that my own company would not give me a concession for $353 of insurance. I signed that form quickly and returned it. I have frequently told that human interest story to convey to tough prospects or rated cases that the system is absolutely fair overall and would not even slightly favor a long time career agent.

I have taken some potshots at the actuaries but once again, I trust them more than I trust any agent to develop a series of rates. When I quote a premium, I don't even think about the fact that maybe a mistake might have been made in calculations and I might do the public a disservice by selling too much of this product. I can imagine the feelings of the actuaries at the continual "actuary" stories and the constant bombardment of requests for better and more competitive products. Along with these pleadings comes the admonishment, "Raise the cash value and the dividends but don't lower the premiums because this lowers the commissions." The constant plaint is to give us something better with which to compete but don't make us as agents pay for it by lower commissions. I wouldn't know how to tackle that problem, but then I never did understand new math.

In the first part of this chapter I took a tough poke at our Home Office counterparts because they were always away from their desks and not available when needed. Now, please consider the problem of the Home Office people when they need a report or some follow-up on a procedure. This is some of the nitty-gritty paperwork of which I spoke. Not all agents complete all records on time. Take, for example, newman activity records. I think if I were training and advancing sizable amounts of money to a person at the same time, I would like to know what that person is doing all the time. I also think the Home Office is entitled to these forms. Some agents say they are so busy making calls they don't have time for keeping records. Yet the results, or even the records themselves when they come in late, don't show a full load of work. When the supervisor calls the agent is "out on appointments." Or when a written request comes to the agent or his unit manager it is often put aside to be done "later" because it is just not priority. The calls or memos are avoided and I can just imagine how frustrating that can be to a training department trying to help the individual by getting an accurate record on where he is weak or where he is strong. And one of the chief violators may be our tenderfoot agent who won't fill out forms but is short of his validation requirements. The Home Office wants records so they can help this man. The records are slow to come and on top of that the general agent wants a special advance because, "He's right on the brink of some good cases. Something big is going to pop from the interviews he has lined up for next week." How can the

Home Office agency supervisor doubt his general agent, yet how can he advance more money without having tangible proof of honest effort? I'm glad I don't have to make those decisions. We can poke fun at the soft jobs the Home Office people have but it takes the wisdom of Solomon and the guts of a Napoleon to call some of these decisions. The opposite of The Forty-One Memo syndrome is the No Response syndrome. One is no better or worse than the other.

The aversion to filling out forms or returning them can, in the final analysis, hurt everyone including the agent or even the client. Like it or not, some of the forms have significance to the policy contract itself. Once a case is issued and the money is in the company accounts, it is only natural that the agent would like to have it in the commission account. But what if there is an amendment form because the application or health application had a blank spot where there should have been a response to a question? The manager also wants credit for a delivered case so he either records it as paid or convinces the Home Office department that the agent will get the form signed tomorrow. He invokes trust and gets his way. We know that only 1 out of 100,000 pieces of mail gets lost but the possible combinations of excuses of, "It's in the mail," are amazing. But this is the life insurance business and claims do occur and it is possible that it could occur during the "excuse" period which could last from the promised one day to months which could accrue. Then what does a claims officer do? The form was never signed and it's not as simple as the TV commercial, "Does she or doesn't she?"

The agents are sometimes thought of by some people as consumers and not producers. We have all been through the one act play called, "Who made the phone call to Los Angeles or New York or anywhere else that we can't account for?" There are certain costs that the agency will pay for and others that it won't. The agent housed in an agency wants to be thought of as a businessman and not an employee. He acts businesslike and efficient when he picks up the black monster to call his good client 3,000 miles away but the business sense and efficiency sometimes fails the memory test when the accounting phase comes into play. He doesn't mean to avoid any costs that are legitimate, he just forgot. The manager trusts his agents but somehow it's always a mystery how experts in the field of financial solvency lose track of who belongs to what charge. It is always a bit comical when the office manager becomes frustrated and vows to get to the bottom of the phantom phone callers. She asks and can't account for every charge on the bill. She calls the phone company and wonders if a mistake could have been made. Eventually, she gives up when the next bill comes in and it's a little smaller. The soothing effect is also faster if the current month happens to be a better production month. In any event, a memo is put our regarding phone procedures that everyone must follow and the hope is that it will work. It does for a little while, then the whole procedure repeats itself.

The same mystery holds true for the photocopy machine. It is humanly impossible to account for every copy that was made in a month. If a television scanner were put on the copy machine, the tooth fairy could still sneak in and make photos that could not be accurately traced. Everyone looks at everyone else and says, "Not me." Another puzzle for which there is no solution is the taking of company records from airtight cabinets. There are always certain areas from which the agents are banned. There are certain records that only office staff can handle. Information must be gotten from them and original records are not to be removed from the front office. So, it's always hilarious when new procedures are installed so the policyholder's virtue is protected. It always works . . . for a while.

"It's not my job," has become the watchword of the specialty or conglomerate or discount department store clerk. It's easy by this negative excuse to completely get out of work or at least put up a smoke screen so the seeker will become turned off and leave. President Harry Truman said, "The buck stops here." So the object is to find the responsible person to facilitate the process from start to finish.

In the two previous sections of this chapter, I've been critical of the actions and attitudes of both Home Office personnel and field personnel. It seems like a classic battle of the cattlemen versus the sheepherders or the officers versus the enlisted men. Is it actually that bad; is there really a rift between the administration and sales forces of companies? The answer is a thundering *NO*. Let's now take a look at the workings of the insurance sales process from the viewpoint of the kid who first came up with the saying, "Tell it like it is."

How it is, is maybe as it should be. As I told my client who said that the Lord will provide, maybe he has. With 250 years of commercial insurance experience and giving full credence to the law of supply and demand and the origin of species, maybe we have arrived at Mecca and don't know it. Even the most hardened agent relies on the phrase, "My

Company" once in a while. Too often it's in time of trouble. Then he is quite willing to shift the burden to the Home Office such as the problem of delivering a rated policy. Then with full sincerity of belonging to a team, he tries to convey to the client that collectively he and the Home Office consider this offer to be a good one. At that moment it's comforting to fall into one mutual effort. But when the agent conveys these feelings in times of trouble, he really means it. They are the true feelings showing through. It then is really a situation of "My Company right or wrong, but My Company."

There is no such thing as a neutral corner. There is nothing about which to be neutral. The process is mutual. Everyone in this process needs the other. If it could be different it would be. If the Home Office could get along without agents, they would. If the field could get along without the Home Office, it would. Therefore, in the unfettered daily relations of the process of application to delivered policy then collecting premiums, if there were a better way, it would be found. In situations such as airline insurance, where no agent is necessary, none is involved. In those cases such as non-medical insurance or guaranteed issue where underwriters are not necessary, none is used. Some companies operate on the general agent basis and others work on the manager basis. Some companies operate on a brokerage only basis and others accept no brokerage. The variances are as wide as might be expected with almost 2,000 companies operating on the basis of capturing a larger part of the market.

Some people on both ends of the product have indicated the difference is wide and "Never the twain shall meet." I don't believe that at all. I think the twain has met. This agency system under which we work is the evolution of everything that has gone before. The input we engender during our careers is the basis of the future of the business. Every business has its cliques, jealousies, feifdoms, peculiarities, backbiting, career-climbing, and even cheating and stealing. We've got it, too. But I know we have it to a lesser degree because the public acceptance of the life insurance business widens each year. Volume isn't the only measure but it's the way we keep score. It sure keeps growing.

Utopian goals would dictate that we get ever closer and try to eliminate any rifts we have. It may never fully materialize but we must keep on trying. One place where we must place the emphasis is squarely in the middle. Certainly the middle in our life insurance business is the liaison between the Home Office and the field. This is the management or general agency corps. I am fully serious when I state my opinion that the future of this business and any form of improvement in relations will come from this group of people. The manager listens to the complaints, ideas, growing pains, and suggestions from both sides and he sorts out in his computer what he should pass on. Sometimes he trades information exactly as he hears it. Sometimes he takes some legal license and edits the information so there will be no hard feelings. Sometimes he embellishes a good idea and makes it better. Sometimes he soothes ruffled feelings. Sometimes he's rough and sometimes he's soft.

The manager is truly what is called a middleman. Some fast-track advertisements talk about cutting out the middleman. We know what we can expect from this kind of operation. Their common thread is direct from low-cost to high-profits and no stop for service in between. In these types of operations the manipulators don't expect to be around tomorrow, therefore, there is no need for service or any other human contact. In our business, everything is promised for tomorrow so we must give service of the highest quality. If we are to take the two views of the impact of what form that service should take, we need someone who can operate somewhat as a hybrid of both of these ends of the insurance business. The Home Office attitude is, "What is best for everybody all the time." The field attitude is, "Yes, but I'm the guy that has to face the client." These views should go hand in hand but in fact they don't always do that. Therefore, a middleman is needed and that person is the manager or the general agent.

If in fact the Home Office methods of operation are exactly right all the time, and if in fact experience and evolution has shown that the best way to merchandise this product is the agent, then there is no choice but to have someone who can understand the job to be done, recruit and train people to do it, and instill a sense of loyalty to all segments of the cadre. In my opinion, the emphasis of the companies should be to train first class quality managers who propagate the system. It may be a slower way than recruiting large numbers of agents, some of whom may succeed and some of whom may fail, however, it seems like the sincerest, most thorough way. Possibly the slowest way is the fastest way. Possibly the quality of recruiting and training could improve by a slower, less pressurized process. For myself, any success I have had in the business is because I was blessed for twenty years, with a dedicated, accessible manager, the late A. G. Billesdon. I, for one, always want an alter-conscience assisting me and currently I am further endowed with a fantastic young general agent, Steven J. Radom.

To summarize this chapter on the dichotomy of philosophies, if any differences do exist between the Home Office and the field, they are minor in the big picture. Further to the point, maybe they're necessary to keep progress going through the process of selective thinking. The whole world and every transaction in it is a competition between the establishment and the disenfranchised. When a flower is squeezed by the vegetation around it, it grows taller to catch the life-giving sunshine before the other plants do. I don't think there is any major conflict occuring between administration and sales so I say, "What establishment? What disenfranchised?"

11

Success—Simplified

Like everybody, I do a certain number of interviews. I sell some, I miss some. MAKE THE CALLS.

12

Simple Simon Says

My primary thrust is the business of telling businessmen how to get out of business . . . "at a profit." The word *profit* is one of the three that the businessman knows the best. The other two are: *wholesale* and *retail*.

My market is the small and medium-sized corporation. I sell business insurance, estate insurance, and retirement insurance to the same guy . . . a business owner. A typical approach follows:

"Mr. Owner, you spend all of your time with your stores wrapped around you. Your entire day is concerned with how to stay in business. You meet with customers to get their business. You hire salesmen to promote your business. You meet with the suppliers to get the materials for your business. You come before anyone in the morning and you stay longer than anyone at night. Even then, you go home with a briefcase under your arm. All with the motive of getting into and staying in business.

"Now comes Meisel with the idea of helping you get out of business . . . at a profit, no less. Someday you will get out, either by death or retirement. This has a cost, as everything does. I'm a supplier and I can do it for you wholesale or more to the point, as every entrepreneur would like to do it . . . with someone else's money."

I tell the businessman that if we complete his business-insurance planning, most times we are well on the way to finishing the whole job.

The estate planning and retirement planning dovetail into the estate planning.

The motive of my entire operation is an attempt at simplifying difficult concepts. Too few of us realize that our product is truly a difficult concept. To reach this goal I try to explain any difficult concept in one word. Think back to our high school English or foreign language studies. Wasn't that the same goal? A noun was defined as a one word noun; an adverb as a one word adverb. Take, for instance, the noun "will." We know for sure that pure Webster says it's "a legal declaration of a persons mind . . . etc." Others may say it's "a method of disposing of property to those people you want to get it."

Tell some of that to a wife or even the businessman with whom you're doing an interview and you may have closed a mind. You started off on a complicated subject that the individual really didn't understand and thought of in his own negative terms. That person could also start thinking of your meeting and the whole subject in the same negative terms. But, if at the first time I mention the word "will" I say that a "will" is nothing more than a "note" I've started the thought processes off in the area of a simple little thing that the individual controls. I then go on to make an analogy to the note a mother would leave for a babysitter, on leaving for a weekend. This note would say, "The doctor's phone number is . . . the fire department's phone number is . . . ; the lady three doors down has a car so if you need anything, she will help out; the refrigerator is full; I left twenty dollars in the cupboard for the cleaners and the paperboy, don't be surprised when they ring the bell on Saturday and if all else fails, here's my mother's phone number, she can be over here in ten minutes."

A trust is a tough thing to understand so we sometimes make our job harder by assuming that our listener really understands what one is. What if he doesn't? Have we closed his mind to everything we may say from here forward? I explain a trust as a "bucket." Every housewife knows what a bucket is and how to get something out of it. She can either turn it over and take everything out, or she can ladle out one dipper at a time.

In this fashion, haven't I just explained the tough concept of a "testamentary disposition using a pour-over will and the marital deduction?" The client and his wife completely understand these mental pictures I have painted for them and wouldn't dare ask me how a "bucket" works. But the costly thing is that for fear of ignorance they also wouldn't ask me to repeat how a "revocable A-B trust" works. With this type of simplicity in the beginning (and hopefully throughout) I can introduce more advanced ideas. If the listener doesn't understand he or she will think the misunderstanding is their fault and not mine. Incidentally, I am a firm believer in having the wife present at all estate planning interviews. I tell her I want to meet her and explain to her in advance what kind of planning her husband and I are doing, and I want to explain it in advance while she's a wife and a beneficiary. I want to do this rather than shock her for the first time with the finality of the story while she's a widow and payee. The mutual trust builds when first off, sufficient time is taken to discuss a complicated subject fully, rather than having the husband come home and announce, "You're taken care of." Secondly, it's been discussed in terms that are understandable. Thirdly, it's discussed as advance planning as opposed to an accomplished fact and "take it or leave it."

BUSINESS INSURANCE

This is the most fun since the terms we use in our jargon are business terms anyway and can be made to parallel the other guy's going concern. Sometimes I get confused with terms such as "stock redemption", "cross purchase", "stock buy-out", "wait and see buy-sell", "stock retirement", and other variations. I just say, "What you need is an umpire." I then explain what an umpire does: he makes decisions based on previous rulings and input. He tries to be fair and favor neither party. I explain that I will work with the owner's other advisors to establish the umpire. The things that a business umpire has to be concerned about are the buyer of the business, the seller, the price, and most importantly, the cash. However, the dominant thing here is "that you fellows can train the umpire to do what you want him to do. If we agree that someday, something is going to have to be done, why not this day when everyone can negotiate for his own best interest and the umpire will have to listen to the final decision that you feed into his rule book. Therefore, when someone steps out of the business, his family isn't "out at home" too. The umpire will be forced to stick by your decisions when he has to make them. Now, like everything in business or anywhere else, there is a price. The umpire has to be paid. It's called legal fees and premiums and they're the cheapest way. When one of

Illustration 12-1

METHODS OF TRANSFERRING BUSINESS INTEREST AT DEATH

	A—RETAIL	B—WHOLESALE
Date of Payment:	After Death	Before Death
Principal Payments on Stock:	Yes	No
Interest Payments:	Yes	Yes
Amount of Principal:	Determined after Death-Subject to negotiations with Heirs, Survivors, Attorneys, IRS, and other Advisors.	Set in advance by Agreement.
Amount of Interest:	Variable-Determined after death-Assume very favorable rate-8%.	3.2%
Actual Cost:	Full value of shares plus interest = 100% interest.	Full value of interest payments paid by date of death. No principal payments. Never reaches 100%.

Timing of Payments:	Start at date of death.	Start discounted payments now. Stop at date of death.
Payments carried on books:	Yes, liability after death for negotiated value of shares.	Yes-Asset before death-For exact equity value of interest payments.
Stock encumbered after death:	Yes	No
Buyer at Death:	Unknown - Not specified.	Corporation
Estate obligated to sell at death:	No	Yes
Discounted value of Principal and Interest available at date of death, in one sum:	No	Yes
Payments waived at disability of Shareholder:	No	Yes

A. Installment payments after death either to heirs or bank, cash if available, reserve account, borrow or any buy now pay later plan.

B. Life Insurance

you dies, everyone listens to this man. The survivor listens, the estate listens, the lawyers listen, and the government listens.

Here I have used only one word: umpire. But I have gone on to explain his duties which fit business just the same way they fit baseball. The key here is the first word which paints a very broad picture. The rest of the words define and refine the idea. Think of the word, "airplane." The word "vehicle" describes the purpose but now the rest of the words will describe its uniqueness.

I find, also, that businessmen like charts and reports so I present them with "charts" and "reports" instead of "proposals" and "ledger sheets." Personally, I find ledger sheets too complicated so I rarely present one. I try to use reports such as the one entitled, "Methods of Transferring Business Interest at Death" (See Illustration 12-1.) Notice the simplicity of shifting eyes from one column to the next. The businessman is used to that. Notice also the words he knows: wholesale and retail. What has this done to his thinking in advance? Any businessman knows wholesale is cheaper than retail, so he likes every point I make on the report. He's preconditioned by words. At the bottom I explain the "A" and "B" legend at the top of the proposal. The "3.2% Amount of Interest" in this case was a compiled premium of two ages where the average premium was $32 per thousand. This also makes an easier job of placing rated cases. I don't have to blame the "premium," I blame the "interest."

RETIREMENT INSURANCE

Pensions are complicated areas. The businessman knows this and he's frightened about the "hassle" before we even start talking, so here is where language means the most. Many times the approach is the close and everything else becomes "exercise," things we have to do to get the government's OK to take a deduction.

I have had the pictured "I GAVE TO THE IRS" button (Illustration 12-2) made up at a cost of $75 per thousand or $.07½ each (deductible). I place this on the prospect's desk, facing me. I don't say anything, just push it a little way towards him. His natural reaction as I'm doing this pushing is to do a little pulling. He reaches out to take it in; at the least, he has to turn it around to read it. If he laughs, puts it on, leaves the room to show it to an associate, make some favorable comment or otherwise indicate acceptance, he has just passed the "eleven second pension" interview.

Illustration 12-2

Think of what has happened if he puts my property on his shirt or coat. He has accepted me and the barriers are down. He agrees that he has given too much to the IRS and he wants to hear the rest of my discussion on one of his favorite dislikes. The body language here tells me that he is receptive.

Let us suppose the opposite happens: He hardly moves, doesn't touch the button, and remains aloof. I now realize that his stiffness is showing; body language that is telling me to work harder. He has now flunked the eleven-second test. So I go further by giving him the minute-and-a-half pension interview.

"Mr. Prospect, I know that your business is open six days a week." As I say this I draw a box, (Illustration 12-3) dividing that into six boxes labeled Monday to Saturday. "No matter how you figure it and no matter what your tax bracket is, when you put together all the state, local, and federal taxes, you're paying 50% of your money in taxes." I've never had anyone disagree; usually it's an affirmative grunt or nod.

At this point, I draw a line between Wednesday and Thursday. "Therefore, you don't really go to work for yourself until Thursday." Now, I usually get a stronger grunt or nod. "I want you to get off the defensive because I'm not talking about your money, I'm talking about Monday's money and that isn't yours, it's the government's. If I ever ask you for a check on Thursday (drawing a check through Thursday), throw me out. Can we go forward?"

Either we go forward or we don't. Just like any other selling, some do and some don't. But I have found this little "Monday's Money" approach is useful to knock down the cool barrier. Once again, simple words take the edge off complicated and scary concepts. If I make common sense at this point, the rest is merely exercise, getting cost and benefit sheets and paper documents. But once engaged the mind is hard to stop, so this is what I've tried to do with concise words, lines, and stories.

Illustration 12-3

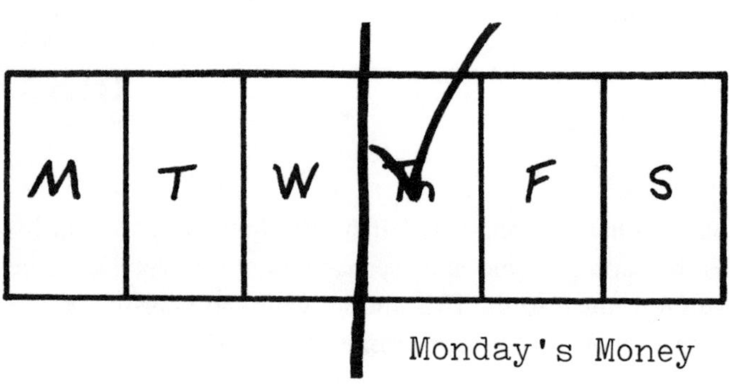

Overall, I try to use the right words and stay away from the wrong words. One of the worst words is "No." I try never to use it, even though sometime I must convey it. I offer two examples:

I do all of my interviews on an "Agenda" format. Most of them take place in my office, using an overhead projector. When giving people agendas, proposals, or papers of any kind, they always look ahead of the items being discussed. I only give out an agenda to allow the people to see it all. If I want them to look ahead, I place the items that I want to emphasize forward in the placement. This way, as the reader sneaks an advance look, he is reading exactly what I want him to see. Then as I come to these items I am doing an extra agenda beyond the actual printed one. My true agenda has been prepared, allowing for the fact that the prospects will be trying to "get ahead" of me.

Here's what I do when I'm handing out a full agenda to clients or prospects in our conference room when I don't want them to look ahead of me and I don't want to instill a negative thought by saying "No" or "Don't look ahead." I give out the complete set of papers. I tell them, "Please look over the complete set." I promptly turn off the light and say, "I have the same material on the acetate overhead, so let's go through it together." No one seems to get upset because I haven't pushed them around with a series of restrictions. In fact, I've asked them to get involved.

You can see that as a great part of my operation I try to use words and ideas rather than numbers and ledger sheets. There are many ways to say the same thing and get the desired result. Some involve extra steps or thoughts which aren't necessary and may bring the wrong result. Consider a freshly painted wall where the painter has put a sign saying "Wet Paint - Do Not Touch." Guess at the result. Think of what's going to happen. Now think of your reaction when you see a sign that instructs you to "do" rather than "not do" something. People like to counter-balance everything as quickly as they can. It's natural to have the computer in your head weigh the opposite side as quickly as possible. I sell to this phenomenon. A painter who was more of a psychiatrist might leave the following sign: "Wet Paint-Wash Hands After Touching." No one wants an extra chore of hand-washing, so they don't touch—all the time thinking, "I'll show that painter. I won't have to take the time to wash my hands." Result? All parties satisfied.

I offer one more small example of the use of just a few words but the right words to suit a service situation which might have blown up and caused a large time-consuming problem. The scene is as follows: Bruce Pension Client calls me on the phone. We'll call him BPC and me IBM (Irwin B. Meisel).

BPC: "Burt, I was talking with my friend about pensions and he told me that I couldn't take my own pension trust money and put it back into my own company. That isn't fair. It's my money. What kind of deal is that? Doesn't the government trust trustees? I'm not doing it now, but what if I wanted to take all my pension money and build a new warehouse. That's a secure investment. I'd give a good interest note. Now why the hell can't I do it?"

IBM: "Calm down, Bruce, you can do it. You may lose all your deductions or go to jail, but you *can* do it."

BPC: "I don't want to go to jail."

IBM: "Don't do it."

BPC: "OK. How's Sharon?" (Change of subject.)

If I had wanted to, I could have explained everything I knew about prohibited transactions, the law before and after ERISA, the 10% limitations, and everything else I could to defend the law. The result would have been a lengthy discussion telling each other how much bureaucracy and red tape we have to live with. He may still have thought it was all my fault because I sold him the pension. This way I gave him choices and he chose the most sensible one because he's a businessman and it cost less. It also cost less in blood pressure.

The words, "deferred compensation" roll off the tongue so easily they sound like poetry. No sensible businessman should say "No" to them. I've done some estate planning with professional athletes who are keenly aware of the benefits of deferred compensation. They know it is a short career and the high pay jammed into a few years results in tax gluttony. Their negotiators know how to put a financial package together to include today's dollars and tomorrow's dollars. I worked with one National Football League player who had deferred compensation agreements from three clubs for whom he had played. Actually it was an interesting case because of the high estate values and the deferred compensation plans starting at age 55 and then 60. This man understood the workings better than any client I have ever met, but generally most people don't understand it well except that it sounds nice and official.

Once we get into the plan fully and if all the factors are right, it fits beautifully and it is one of the best fringe benefits around. But sometimes it's difficult to get across the concept unless we get early interest from the listener. For years I have used "An Exchange Of Promises" (Illustration 12-4) to get quick attention to the concept. Most times, the plan can be sold right from the one sheet. Other times it requires more back up such as computer illustrations. Who can resist an exchange of promises, especially if it is between yourself and a company that you control. The illustration is for $75,000 of permanent insurance. The only items that ever need changing are the seven numbers. Items 1 and 2 under "Corporation Promises" are simply the terms of the agreement. Item 3 is the monthly premium.

Item 2 under "Rights of Parties - Corporation" is the highest difference between premiums paid and guaranteed cash value. You will find this under the "Net Cost" column of the policy ledger statements (not shown.) For example, if the total premiums in the seventh year were $15,434 and the cash value was $10,000, the total cost is $5,434. This is the most the corporation can ever lose because if it surrenders after this point, the net cost is decreasing. Of course is pays more but the cash value must be carried on its books as an asset. If it surrenders, it gets back its asset. Either way, the only cost is the difference in premiums and cash value.

Item 1 under "Obligations of Parties - Corporation" is the monthly premium again. I find that this sheet explains the basic concept and implants the idea in the "desire" column and only pertinant facts have to be explained by referring back to the basic promises, rights, and obligations.

Illustration 12-4

DEFERRED COMPENSATION
(An Exchange of Promises)

CORPORATION PROMISES:	IF	EXECUTIVE PROMISES:
1. To continue $15,000 salary for 5 years after retirement.		1. To remain with corporation until age 65.
2. If Executive should die before retirement, continue $15,000 salary to family for 5 years.		2. Not to compete with corporation after retirement.
3. Corporation will set aside $225 per month in sinking fund.		3. Be available for consultation after retirement.

RIGHTS OF PARTIES

CORPORATION	EXECUTIVE
1. Right to use sinking fund for any other proper corporate use. This includes borrowing, investing, pledging, etc.	1. No change from present.
2. Corporation reserves right to limit total cost of promise to $5,434.00.	

OBLIGATIONS OF PARTIES

CORPORATION	EXECUTIVE
1. Place $225 per month with Fiduciary.	1. No change from present.

13

They

They say . . . They say falling in love is wonderful. They say California is going to break off and fall into the ocean. They say that Good Friday is going to be celebrated on Monday so there can be a longer holiday weekend. They say taxes are going up. They say taxes are going down. They say haste makes waste. They say he who hesitates is lost.

"Step on a crack, break your mother's back." Who says so? They say . . . Did you hear they found Adolph Hitler in South America? "Who says?" "They said." "Where did you hear that?" "Everyone is saying that." "Who's everyone?" "You know." "Seriously, where did you hear that?" "I heard it more than one place." "Where?" "I don't remember but I know I heard it from someone reliable."

I think all of us have heard the above dialogue in one form or another at some time. Probably most of us have been on the "saying" side of the conversation at times. It's easy to propound either side of a theory if you're not really involved and what better way to do it than by declaring, "They say." This way if the idea strikes a responsive positive tone, it's easy to take credit for it. If it's questioned or proven wrong, it's also easy to back off by blaming it on a far away, anonymous person or persons unknown. It's also easy to completely repudiate the statement by saying, "I never believed it in the first place."

Saying "they" also can be a great defensive tactic when one is not willing to take responsibility. "They" can also be anyone you haven't met, such as "my lawyer," "my banker," "my CPA" "my parents," "my children," "my friend," "my car pool," and even "our babysitter." I once sold a young couple a family policy with a decreasing term rider. The total coverage was $45,000 and the total premium was $20 a month. When I called to deliver the policy the husband told me he didn't want it. I asked him why and he told me that his babysitter told him that I lied because insurance wasn't that cheap. This was in the days before the ten day free look, but in any event I wanted to get to the bottom of this to find out who was this babysitter who was calling me a liar.

I told him, "You've already paid a monthly premium so you are going to have sixty days of coverage. You might as well take delivery of the policy and find out exactly what you do have for protection." I slowly and carefully detailed the policy to them before I asked any questions regarding the babysitter. When I finished he said, "I'll take it."

I replied, "Good, but tell me about the babysitter." It turned out that the babysitter was a sixty-five year old woman whose husband had just recently applied for $2,500 of insurance for about the same $20 figure. It was her contention that $20 only bought $2,500 of coverage regardless of what type of coverage or age of the insured.

In this case, I was able to deal with the situation because I was able to get right to the source of the information. I found "they." Many times in our relations with people we can't find or meet "they." Sometimes because there is no one, and sometimes because we're not permitted to meet them. I have also had the experience of an enthusiastic buyer becoming negative after talking to some other advisor. When I got all the facts I found that the client did not explain all of the details to the other party. Or sometimes, the other party simply has a different viewpoint because all sides of the transaction were not able to communicate with each other. Other times the other so-called advisor will only give a viewpoint based on a narrow set of facts having to do with his area only. The CPA or attorney should feel very nervous about giving advice in the insurance area without having a meeting with the agent and client present. By nature the lawyer has a very narrow scope with which he deals with the client. He almost never vigorously brings up insurance unless the client first prods him with thoughts of estate or retirement or business planning. The same is true of the CPA, banker, trust officer, or other professional. The insurance man, on the other hand, coordinates many areas touching on all of the professions and as a catalyst, stimulates action.

It's rare that I would ever actively tell a client that his attorney or CPA is dead wrong and should be fired. But all of us have had this happen to us when the client is contacted after a meeting and tells us, "My lawyer says don't do it." The advisor has just said, "Fire the insurance man." Recently I told a client, in just this sort of situation, to fire his attorney. His response was disbelief. "Did you say I should fire him?"

"Yes."

"Why?"

"He said fire me and unless I oppose him vigorously and resist, in effect I'm agreeing with him by saying that my proposal had no merit. I do not withdraw my idea because if I did I would be saying that I was thinking of me and not you when I made it. This is not the case. I firmly believe the solution that I recommended is needed. So I say, 'Fire your attorney and hire me.' "

The client said he appreciated my sincerity and wanted to think for a couple of days. He then called his attorney who finally called me, although previously he hardly ever returned my phone calls.

"Mr. Meisel, did you say fire me?"

"Yes."

"Why?"

"Because if everything is just as Mr. B______ said, you don't know what you're talking about."

"Do you realize that you're bordering on practicing law?"

"No, I didn't realize that but if you're referring to my work on this case, that's what I do everyday. If that's practicing law, then I'm practicing law. One of us has to do it."

There was a silence on the phone until the attorney said, "Pretty sure of yourself, aren't you?"

I said, "On this case, yes. Are you sure of what you advised on this case or is it possible that you didn't hear the full case development because I wasn't at the meeting. Unless you want to argue some more, I suggest you and I get together and listen to each other's reasoning."

He said, "OK, but I'm not coming to your office, you'll have to come to mine." I did meet with him and we agreed the insurance should be placed just the way it was proposed. The client was much happier when he heard that we both met and came to the same conclusion. I was fortunate in this case to have an attorney with enough guts to meet after the phone confrontation. Most times when it goes that far, the client would feel uncomfortable in bucking the lawyer's advice. However, I have found it effective to say, "Fire the lawyer." At least that conveys credence to your ideas and conviction to back up your thinking.

Not only is "they" individuals with whom we work but, most assuredly in these times, we also have to be concerned with the big "THEY" spelled in capitals because it comes primarily from the capitol, government agencies. Along with government agencies we have to consider consumer groups. The Federal Trade Commission and other investigative committees have done the public no favor in showing a one-sided approach to the cost of life insurance. There is no reason that a life insurance policy, either term or permanent, should be compared in first year cost only. It's unfair not to study the total cost for the projected life expectancy or some long time into the future such as twenty or thirty years. To do otherwise would not even be considering "life" insurance; the thought would be "death" insurance. This has been the primary thrust of the FTC report since the implication is to "get the best bargain." This implies the client should die early. I'm surprised they haven't recommended to buy term insurance and pay monthly. This way the payor would never have too much money invested in a policy.

When the FTC report was nearing completion in 1978, I wrote to the author of the report with copies of my letter going to President Carter and about fifteen members of Congress. I got back about twenty-five letters from people I had not written or people I had never heard of. Mostly these people were aides of the Congressmen who basically sent me a commercial thanking me for my interest and telling me that my thoughts would be taken under advisement. I received a letter from the President's office saying the same thing. What happened is that the people I wrote gave the job of responding to their "theys." The result was that I got the exercise of explaining my viewpoint but my input didn't have one iota of importance. The FTC report came out just as the investigative people wrote it and the furor it caused is history. The report was basically an indictment of permanent insurance. It made a prominent display in all the newspapers and television. The newspapers dwelled on the "alleged" low interest return on the permanent insurance but the follow-up explanations weren't as openly explained. *The Phil Donohue Show* on television at least gave equal time to members of both sides of the opinion.

However, the damage was done. "They" had won out again. It was amazing to me how fully the doomsayers had read the report. It verified for many people the "negative" aspects of life insurance. The good part of it all is that "this too, shall pass away." The overall good of the life insurance product will win out in the final analysis since it is truly the supply of the public's demand.

I remember back in the mid 1960's when "they" said the mutual funds were the wave of the financial future. "They" said life insurance was doomed. Insurance men were worried; they quickly studied for the investment licenses. I took the philosophy that if so many people were going to be the "full financial planners" there was still going to be a solid place for the specialist who knew a lot about his product and was solid, as opposed to the man who knew a little bit about a lot of things and was an opportunist. The mutual fund domination folded quickly and life insurance endured. I personally never became licensed to sell funds and I advised my friends to continue to study and specialize. The same advice still prevails today. Panic about inflation and "investing the difference" will pass and the absolute safety of the marriage of compound interest and the mortality table will go on at least another 250 years. The problem with life insurance is that it is so simple it's hard to believe. It's so safe that to some people it's dangerous. "They" can't stand the simplicity so the efforts to "improve" the policyholder's position only improves the "transplant artist's" position. But as always, rape is only a temporary pleasure that ultimately does neither party any good.

One of the real problems is that most of the "theys" don't create anything new. "They" raid existing cash values. "They" project wonderful gains; the possible losses are minimized by referring to some "fair cross section" time frame during which there were highs and lows but the results were eventually, up. Most of these plans are of the "split dollar" arrangement in that "they" split the client from his dollars. In 1973, I had a phone call from a client explaining to me the wild and wondrous virtues of changing all of his policies to term insurance and investing the difference in the market with a "consultant'' who had come to his house. The salesman obviously painted a beautiful picture of steady growth and vast improvement over the present program.

The client was a 49-year old man who worked as an engineer for one of the utility companies. He always made a slightly above-average income but he had nine children, four of whom were still at home. Therefore, even though his income was not meager, the family size did not leave room for more than standard minimum living conditions. He was one of my first clients in 1956 when I sold him a family policy. Through the years he managed to get to a $50,000 whole life program by $5,000 and $10,000 increments. His cash value was about $9,000 which represented almost all of his savings in the world. The agent had appealed to the client's desire for more return and to his gullibility; and maybe even a little greed. By the time Tim had called me, there was no doubt his mind was made up. Even though he said he wanted to discuss his policies, there was nothing to discuss. He knew what he was going to do. People first make up their minds and then find reasons to justify the decision. When he explained the program to me he said it was not a quick decision, after all "This is the kind of insurance the company has for me and I went to the library and got a book on term insurance. It's better for me."

I suggested he sell his home and rent an apartment and invest the difference in this same medium. If it paid as well as he was projecting by age 65 he would have enough cash to buy the whole complex. He protested that he wouldn't mess with the equity in his home, but he didn't want to accept my analogy regarding the equity in his policies. He said he wanted to surrender all policies and buy term insurance from me. I told him I wouldn't sell him the term insurance because I disagreed with this entire transaction and I didn't want any part of it. I also told him I would not service the policies during the surrender transaction. I would not send him surrender forms nor would I witness them. I didn't want my name connected with this mistake, in any way. I further indicated to him that he was entitled to this service so if he wanted to complain about me to the home office he could, but I was finished speaking on this subject.

In Michigan, we have replacement forms to be completed in policy replacement situations. When the forms came in for the surrenders, I looked them over. Literally, the only accurate items for the six policies were the policy numbers. The rest of the comparison items were not even completed. Six policies were represented on one form. It was impossible to get that much writing on the form, let alone accounting for different cash values, dividends, contestability periods, etc. All the values were lumped together and inaccurate. I couldn't stand the swindle so I did call the other agent who said to me, "Tim H. is a jerk, I don't even know why I deal with him. The state only says I have to complete the form, not be accurate. If he signs the form, that's all that is required."

I dropped any further conversation at that point since it was now substantiated to me that this agent only had an enlightened self-interest and only cared about his commission on both products, and not one bit for the client. Pitifully, Tim was just in time for the 1974-75 recession. The $9,000 cash value dwindled to $2,000 and the term increased in premium right on schedule. His wife, Betty, called me in late 1975, crying and wondering if there was any way to reverse the procedure. I told her there was but all the cash value plus interest and medical evidence had to be provided. They didn't have the $7,000 needed. This, too, is one of the tragedies of this type of theft; the client is the one who can least afford it. The natural prey of the unnatural salesmen is the modest, unsophisticated client. The very guy who needs the best, most sincere service is the guy who is the pigeon of the dollar-splitting hustler. The larger, more sophisticated policyowner at least has some knowledge of investments and access to lawyers and CPAs. In addition, if he happens to make a bad investment, either he could take his losses or alternatively stick with the depressed investment until it rebounds. Sometimes greed is the ally of "they."

So far in this chapter I have spoken in the negative about "they." But there is a completely different side to the good, legitimate advisors of our clients. These fine professionals are the ones that we most frequently meet when working for a sophisticated client who has made his estate large by relying on the good judgment of a quality agent. It's a pleasure to meet with other professionals who are competent in their area and confident enough not to feel threatened by quality planning from a quality insurance agent. The same holds true in reverse for us agents when working with these advisors. People are people, and we make as many false judgments and threatening incursions as the rest of the aides do.

A good life underwriter does not draft legal documents. He also does not do accounting books. The lawyer and accountant, by the same log-

Illustration 13-1

RELATIONS WITH OTHER PROFESSIONALS

PROFESSIONAL	GOAL	CONTACT CONDITION	ATTITUDE	COMMUNICATIONS
Doctor	Action Reaction Reciprocal	Seeker Provider	Negative	Slow
Lawyer	Same	Same	Positive Negative Mutual	Slow Copies
Banker	Same	Same	Positive Mutual	Fast Copies
Trust Officer	Same	Same	Same	Fast Copies
Accountant	Same	Same	Positive Negative Mutual	Fast Copies
CPA	Same	Same	Same	Fast Copies
Bookkeeper	Same	Provider	Negative	Slow
Professional Manager	Same	Seeker or Provider	Negative	Medium Copies
Government Agencies	Action Reaction	Provider Seeker	Positive Negative	Slow
Insurance Agents	Action Reaction Reciprocal	Seeker Provider Reciprocal	Positive Negative	Fast or Slow
Home Office Personnel	Action Reaction Reciprocal	Seeker Provider	Negative Positive Mutual	Slow
Our Secretaries	Same	Reciprocal	Mutual	Fast
Other Persons Staff	Same	Seeker Provider	Positive Mutual Negative	Fast to Slow

ic, do not have the right to advise in the insurance area. They just are not qualified. Nor are we qualified to go into court. And the fact of the matter is the truly professional advisor doesn't infringe on our area. He helps when he is called into a case, on the proper basis. And the proper basis is a purely business relationship. We all need each other for the specific talents in specific fields. But have you ever thought of all of the professionals we deal with on a daily basis? Most of these people don't have degrees or letters behind their names but we vitally need them in order to smoothly carry out our functions. Please refer to the chart. It

REFERRALS	LENGTH OF RELATIONSHIP	REMUNERATION	CENTERS OF INFLUENCE
No	Short	No	Yes
Yes	Long	1. Occasional Lunch 2. Referrals	Yes
Yes Infrequently	Short	No	No
Same	Short	No	No
Yes	Long	1. Occasional Lunch 2. Football Tickets 3. Referrals	Yes
Yes	Long	Same	Yes
No	Short	No	No
No	Short	No	No
No	Short	No	No
No	Long to Short	No	No
No	Long	Cheery Communications	No
Yes	Short	1. Pay 2. Occasional Lunch 3. Christmas Gift 4. Day Off	Yes
No	Short	No	No

---

shows who these people are and on what basis we deal with them. (See Illustration 13-1).

Looking at the list, you will easily recognize some of the people with whom we deal and consider as professionals such as the doctor, lawyer, and accountant. But, I point out to you that everyone else on that list is as professional as the other and all of them are very important to us. Too many businessmen take the home office liaison people for granted. The same holds true for the staff people of other colleagues with whom we work. However, I think the most important people with whom we work and who sometimes don't get the respect they deserve are our own secretaries.

I don't think any of us would like to overhear a conversation in which we are referred to as "that guy." Yet to my mind and to the minds of most secretaries the all time leading slander is the phrase "the girl." When spoken in just the right tone with a slightly "better than thou" attitude it denotes "slave." I think it is the same disgust with which black men perceive the term, "boy." Probably, on occasion, the first time a good secretary hears the phrase, "the girl" come out of the executive's mouth is the same time she records the warning flag to herself that she's not appreciated and she had better keep her eyes open for a new job where she would be happier. Her ears have already told her that "there is no more joy in Mudville" with this one. Think about the person who associates his secretary with a piece of furniture or the extension of the typewriter and at the same time think of the thoughts that go through your mind when you hear "they say." These ladies have names, whether they prefer the first or the last, but more important, they have feelings. They are proud of the work they do and for the most part, consider themselves as a vital part of the organization. I couldn't get along without my secretaries. They're good and I hope they stay forever. Replacing and retraining is one of the world's worst tasks. So when I think of the professionals with whom I deal, first and foremost are the professionally trained ladies on my staff who keep me going down the path to worthwhile efforts and production, and they do it by keeping me in the right frame of reference. I'm the salesman and they are the secretaries, and that is how I refer to them.

To explain the chart I have made, (Illustration 13-1) let's refer to the line entitled "Our Secretaries." Under "Goal" I want to relate the purpose with which we deal with this professional, whether we want action or we are reacting to someone else's request, or if it's reciprocal and we're working together. For the secretary, you'll notice that usually we seek the action. We stimulate the procedures and we start her in the processes. Secondly, at other times we are reacting to their action such as providing more information for the underwriting departments with which she's working. She'll come to us for our help when we are the ones that have to do the work. On other occasions the goal is mutual, and I've labeled the order of action in the most frequent sequence such as action, reaction, and reciprocal. You will notice that mostly this is the same order that we deal with most people. We're usually asking that someone else do something.

The column entitled "Contact Condition" shows the usual order under which we contact these people, either as a seeker or provider. In most cases we are the seeker, once again indicating the nature of our work. Taking the secretary as an example, you see that the purpose is reciprocal. We have a mutual interest in getting the business done.

Under the column, "Attitude" let's look at "Home Office Personnel." Usually the attitude is negative, although it is not too far from positive. It's a somewhat reluctant compliance. It should be mutual but in reality most requests seem to be a disturbance of a pre-programmed routine.

The "Communications" column is self-explanatory.

Whether or not we can get "Referrals" from these people is obvious.

The "Length of Relationshp" is also obvious.

Under "Remuneration" I have listed whether or not we pay these people or in what form. Take the "Accountant" for example. I have listed an occasional lunch, or football tickets, or referrals. I don't always pick up the tab when I go to lunch. Sometimes I pay; sometimes the other party pays; sometimes, but rarely, we split the tab. It depends on how the basis developed. Usually the one who is the seeker does the paying. If it is someone with whom I have lunch often, I pick up one tab and if there is an attempt by the other party to get it I say, "You get the next one," and we alternate. If the other party makes a genuine effort to get it, I let him and say, "The next one is on me." I don't believe we have to sponsor everyone for everything in order to present a purely business situation. Sometimes before the meal, in order to keep the lines of communication unblemished, I'll say, "Just so there is no jostling later on let's agree now that we'll split the check." This also relieves the other guy if he wasn't sure if he should pay it or not. As you can see, there is no set pattern, just doing what truly comes natural.

We have a routine for giving out football tickets that gets double and sometimes triple duty. We don't offer tickets for the Saturday game until Wednesday. The odds are that a call at that late time will get a "Sorry, can't make it but try me again." It may take as many as five calls until the tickets are unloaded. But the important thing is that offering is just as good as giving. The gesture itself is well thought of.

The best way we can pay our professional colleagues is by giving them referrals when we can. It is just as important to them to get a new client as it is to us. However, just as it's tough to get a steady flow of names from them because they deal with so many insurance men, it's tough to have enough names to give an abundance of names to any one professional. In the same way they tell us that most of the clients already have insurance agents, most of our clients already have advisors. Besides, we want to spread the goodwill as much as we can among as many as we can.

People are people and the world is round. Treat everyone as you would want to be treated yourself. You can't do any good or harm in this world without it coming back to you, in kind. This may be the most even form of deferred compensation. We never know when or on what basis we are going to meet someone in the future so lay the good, positive groundwork now. Appreciate the other person's feelings and position in every transaction, and your only surprises in the future will be good ones. And when "they" say something about you in the future, "they" may say something good.

14

Don't Fence Me In

When the new man comes into the insurance business he is trained in the various areas of technical and common sense transactions. One of the methods he is taught is the use of human interest stories. He is told what an effective method it is in relating to people things for which they can have an actual feeling. The clinical stories of the application of insurance principles to people's problems can sound like a sales track unless it is truly felt by the teller. Then, there is nothing that can thwart the power of sincere truth. It wills out all the time. The kids have the saying, "Tell it like it is." They're right. We all know when the heavy words of truth are laid upon us, it is disarming but the kindest, quickest, most efficient way of communication, even if the message isn't good news. The old mythology king's method of "kill the messenger if you don't like the message" doesn't apply. The truth won't go away.

I want to relate a human interest story now that is completely, nakedly the truth. It is a human interest story of two families brought together to be the closest of friends and business confreres all because of the meeting during an insurance transaction. I have permission of my closest friends to tell this story publicly and use their names. The story contains a fantastic number of human interest twists that I have lived and felt along with my good friends.

I first met Larry Traison after I came into the insurance business in 1956. We met as members of a B'nai Brith lodge chapter, newly formed in Detroit. Shortly thereafter I met Larry's wife, Barbara, at lodge functions or social events. In the fall of 1956, Larry and I set up an appointment to talk about life insurance. We made the appointment for an evening at the upper flat where Barb and Larry lived. I can remember, even today, the cold attitude as I walked into the flat. Barbara was unhappy that we were having this appointment and was dead set on Larry not paying money for anything. It was an uncomfortable meeting with her letting us know, in no uncertain terms, that she was unhappy. She wouldn't join us but busied herself in the kitchen, all the time keeping an ear on us.

Larry was working for his father in the family printing business called Walker Printery. The business got its name from the fact that Larry's father, Sam, either didn't own a car in the early days of the business or only did work for the customers which were close to the shop. Please remember, those were the days when Americans went to the store. Nowadays, with strip centers and shopping malls being built on every vacant piece of land, the shopping comes to us. Sam was a kind, generous man who did work gratis for the local synagogue and subscribed to all charities that came through the door. Like father, like son, Larry has always done the same and has gone through the chairs in his congregation and next year will be president. But Sam ran a small business that just made a living and walked the jobs to the customers for delivery. He took so much kidding about his walking that he took that as the name of his shop, Walker Printery.

On the night of this first interview, Larry and I talked about $10,000 of permanent insurance with a family income rider of about $35,000, with a total premium of about $18 per month. Larry wanted the plan but Barb said, "No." They were in the process of applying for a mortgage on their first home. The cash was carefully accounted for and this $18 per month was exactly the amount that was needed for a fence from Sears. The fact that a new mortgage was in the picture made the insurance more necessary but Barb was firm in her committment of "No." A serious debate went on between Larry and Barb and I was sure there was no sale and I was only anxious to get out of the house. Finally, it was agreed to think over the policy for a couple of weeks, then discuss it again. I was sure the fence had won. Larry opened the front door for me and said, "Call me at the shop tomorrow." I did and he bought. For a long while after that Barb only spoke to me when necessary and in the fewest possible words.

In early 1957, I visited Larry at the shop and we set up another policy just like the first, giving him a total of $20,000 permanent and $70,000 term. The big feature was that I programmed out the term so that it would give Barbara $400 per month in addition to Social Security. The reason the family income was so vital was the birth of their daughter, Sheri, in August, 1956. My daughter, Bonnie, was born ten days before Sheri and the girls have always been close friends. As a matter of fact, they went on a European trip together and were roommates in their first year at Michigan State University. By this time, the Traisons were in their new home in Southfield, Michigan, without a fence. Barb often reminded me about the fence and said I was the cause of their not having it.

In September, 1957, Sam Traison died. When the estate was totaled it had $15,000 more liabilities than assets. Larry called me in a very low mood and said he may be out of a job. We discussed what he would do since printing was the only job he knew. I asked what was the make up of the debts. He told me that it was substantially a $57,000 paper bill to one supply house. I was only in the business fifteen months and had never sold anything over a $25,000 policy much less wander into the twilight zone of business insurance. I had just read some "science-fiction" stuff about debtor-creditor insurance so with nothing to lose and, truthfully, not knowing the full details of what I was talking about, I made a suggestion to Larry.

He had told me he knew he could run the business but he needed some cash; about $15,000. I told him he should suggest to the paper supplier that they loan him $15,000 and he would sign a note for $72,000, thereby taking over his father's debts and at the same time offering a chance for recovery. I told him further to suggest that the owner of the supply house buy $72,000 of insurance on Larry to guarantee that if Larry should die the debt would be repaid. He was scared to make the approach but I was brave since I didn't have to do the talking. I spurred him on. When he called me the next day, he didn't have to use words; the joy exuded through the phone wires. The supply house thought it was a good idea. Within two days I wrote the application and Larry got his cash. I also got a new client, the paper supply house.

In the next couple of years we did no additional insurance business because he was financially locked in to the shop. But those were the days of two and three percent inflation and the needs stayed fairly constant. Son Steve was born in June of 1959 and in April of 1960 we set up savings type policies on both Sheri and Steve. By this time I was a little more welcome at the Traison home because of the events of a month earlier. Barb still reminded me that they didn't have a fence but she was joking about it now.

In March of 1960, Larry went to the bank to borrow money to buy a collater which is a machine that puts sheets of various sized printed material into glued sets. This was something that most small print shops didn't have in those days but he felt would add a new dimension of expansion to Walker Printery's ability. He needed $13,500. The banker was going over the statement when he thought Larry had made a mistake because it said $80,000 of life insurance. Larry told him that he took this right off a summary sheet I had given him. The banker talked about something else then came back saying, "Are you sure this isn't a typing error and is only $8,000 of insurance?"

Larry said, "Now you've got me wondering. I thought it was $80,000; but now I'm not sure. Why don't you call my agent?"

The banker said, "OK, if you'll give me your permission."

When the banker called, I was in. He explained the situation and let me talk to Larry. He told me to give the banker any information he wanted. He asked the simple question. "How much insurance does Mr. Traison have?"

"$80,000," I answered.

The banker replied "Thanks" and hung up. He then explained to Larry that his credit record was very young and the past business history wasn't the strongest, but was immensely impressed with the foresight and planning that Larry had in setting up such a large insurance program. He liked the trend of things and granted the loan. He did ask that $13,500 of insurance be assigned to the bank because on death they didn't want the machine, they wanted cash. Larry called to thank me for the help once again. I told him when next I saw Barbara I would remind her, before she got to me, that they still didn't have a fence but she had a collater. I've always thought that it was a lucky thing that Larry ran into a banker who had the standard bank $10,000 group insurance and not a complete program.

Now, a collater is a machine that must have large jobs to make it possible to make a profit. When I first saw it, I thought it was the forerunner of modern automation. It worked fairly non-profit until September of that year when the financial turning point came. Larry got a call from the purchasing agents of one of the auto divisions in Detroit. The PA explained, in bosslike fashion, that his usual source had broken down and he had a great number of sets that needed collating by Monday morning. This was Friday afternoon and Larry was on the launch pad and knew it. He assured the purchasing agent that he had a staff to do the job and it could be finished by Monday morning. He lied.

Later that afternoon trucks arrived with pallets of printed material and a few hand-constructed sets. Larry called other printers for additional people who would help his staff work around the clock all weekend. Anyone who wouldn't work was fired. They ate and slept at the shop. Promptly at 9 am on Monday the PA called. Was the job ready? Larry said, "No."

"How much is?"

"About half."

"Good. I didn't think you'd have that much. When can I have the rest?"

"By Wednesday afternoon."

"Can I pick up the finished ones right away?"

"Yes."

"Thank you."

Larry has had that contract ever since and he'll tell anyone who will listen that it all started with an adequate insurance program. As for Barbara, still no fence, but a Thunderbird convertible. (In the days when a Thunderbird was a Thunderbird!)

In the next few years, as business prospered, we added more insurance. Also during those years, he made policy loans to buy more machinery. In 1968, Larry underwent very serious surgery from which he recovered nicely but left him uninsurable. I truly felt heavy-handed on the day I visited both Larry and Barbara at the shop shortly after his return to work; they wanted to talk about the insurance. I didn't like the appointment because, even though we had options, there was no choice. As all of you know, when we have to look the insurance purpose square in the eye, there is no compromise. We say what we have to say and there is no stroking. It was at this interview that Barbara said, "Please explain to us what we have and what we should do." I explained the summary sheet to two very attentive listeners. When I was finished, it was Barbara who said, "How much of a monthly premium to convert all of that term?" I figured the answer and she said, "Do it."

In 1972, we installed a fully insured defined-benefit pension plan. The case was small enough so there was no guaranteed issue and Larry's benefit came from an annuity, but no death benefit. In 1976, I tried to get insurance for him but still the companies said, "Two more years." Last year I was able to get additional insurance for Larry at standard rates. It was a happy day for all of us.

In 1978, Steve finished his printing studies at Ferris State University and came to work for Larry full time. He reminds me of the young Larry of twenty-four years ago. His energy and talent are the same and his father is as proud as can be. Steve has started his own insurance program on a high level and I'm pleased to be involved with this third generation business. As a result of the most recent estate planning, we are establishing a sizeable insurance policy for Larry owned by Steve. The purpose is to give Steve the business, give Barbara the full estate for her lifetime use, and make equal distributions under the marital and family trusts.

Barbara said to me just a few days ago that this story about two young, penniless boys going their own ways in separate businesses, helping each other to succeed would be a worthwhile chapter in my book. Barb, you're right! Neither one of us got fenced in because we have the desire to dream and the desire to work. I worked so hard I have a fence at my house but nothing will ever fence out the love my family has for the Traison family.

15

The Rest of the Story

Our business has been likened to a game. It has been likened to the theatre with the salesmen the performers, the clients the audience, and the applause the pay, It has been likened to all forms of business such as wholesale-retail, discounted dollars, accounts payable, depreciation of income as retirement plan dollars, raw product—by product, and all other forms of ingenious ideas that salesmen originate. Also, the ideas will never stop. We feed and grow off each other. New, young agents come along and see the elbow sticking out from the usual way of presenting our product and devise new, intriguing stories that fascinate the client and become very understandable to him. Our business has also been designated as the purest form of love next to religion. It's been called social security for the rich and the salvation of the poor.

But there is only one thing that it is, pure and simple: money when it's needed. The result of all the exercise, the bottom line, the rest of the story: money when it's needed. The bottom line!

Just as it is the last chapter of this book, I will relate a story that typifies the insurance purpose by being the last chapter of the insurance purpose. But even then it goes beyond to even bigger benefits. Pay attention and be proud.

In 1966 I was a full time branch manager and agent for the Canada Life Assurance Company. I was in Lansing, Michigan for a meeting with the trustees of a pension plan for a discount drug chain which had stores throughout lower Michigan. The plan was a defined benefit pension plan which had an anniversary date of May 1. We had been trying to get together since May but because of the problems of time and a very busy, profitable year, it was not until this date that the three trustees and I could meet. We held the meeting on the morning of December 12, 1966. The plan was amended to increase benefits by approximately 40%, back to May 1.

For the three trustees, the increases in insurance were sizable and the medical examinations were arranged by telephone right at that meeting. For the other employees all of the insurance increases were of a size that fell within the range of guaranteed issue so none of the employees required physical examinations. All of their insurance would be issued under a group insurance philosophy. All that was required were the applications signed by the trustees and the employees. All of the applications were completed in full except for the signatures of the employees. Some of the applications were left with the trustees to get the signatures and some I took with me to see the people in cities that I could get to. I left Lansing and drove the 70 miles back to Grand Rapids.

Late that afternoon I got a phone call from one of the trustees who asked if everything we had done was completed and in effect. He was very nervous and I asked him what was the matter. His response was, "Ben had a heart attack." Ben was one of the store managers in one of the cities where I would have been the next day to get employee's signatures. I asked if there was any sign of how serious the attack was and he told me it appeared very serious. He then asked me if the insurance was in force and I told him, "No." His response was that it should be since the policy would be guaranteed issue. I explained that the trust document was the umpire and detailed very carefully that neither the trustees, corporation, nor insurance company was under risk for insurance which was not yet in force. This policy was obviously not in force since Ben had not yet signed the application and it appeared it would be some time until he could.

The trustee told me that it was the feeling of all the trustees that all the employees' policies should be in force from the time of the signing of the resolution, signing of applications by trustees, and the issuance of a check. They did understand that medical examination applications were not in force. But it was their firm intention that this particular policy was. This was obviously not a very pleasant situation or conversation for either of us. I told him the best thing we could do was wait a while and see how Ben progressed. He was not fully satisfied that I could not agree with his reasoning but we had no choice but to wait. I was very nervous and could not sleep well that night.

The next morning I was extremely anxious to call and find out how Ben was doing but held off making the call hoping that, for the moment, no news was to be taken as good news. It wasn't too late in the morning when the phone call came and the message was just as clear, concise, and ominous as all claim calls come. Three words, "Burt, Ben died." Now there was no more speculation and no more chance for improvement of the situation. There was no chance that something in between was possible. Either a claim was going to be paid or it wasn't.

I told the trustee that I would call the pension department of the home office and verify exactly what the position of the insurance company was. This was the first pension plan I had ever sold and I was hoping that I was novice enough to have missed something. I made the call and got switched two or three times by persons who wouldn't say out loud what they knew, that no claim was payable.

Finally, I was switched to Phil Pepper, CLU who said the words out loud, "Burt, we have no legal way of paying this claim, the trustees have no obligation to pay this amount and the corporation is under no obligation to pay." I knew that all the time but now it was official, an officer of the insurance company had said what I knew was right. Phil did say that he would refer the situation to the legal department and take the trust document to them to read. I asked him to please do it quickly and please implore them to give the case the best possible interpretation.

This obviously was a bad time for me, a bad time for the trustees who were extremely honorable and loyal employers, but most of all a rough time for Ben's family although at this time thoughts of insurance hadn't even come to their minds. At this moment, I didn't want to call the trustees back to even mention my conversation. I would have liked to have forgotten the whole incident but that's not the way of life. I stalled for a short while thinking I would get a quick phone call from the home office saying that there was a binding obligation and reason to pay.

After a tense hour, I picked up the phone to call the home office. I was switched to Tom Walsh, the top legal officer in the company. He laid it out very plainly—no claim payment to be made. I argued, I pleaded, and I sold, all to no avail. No claim!

I sat dejectedly for a while, then called the trustees. I did not tell them there was no payable claim. I told them the home office was still looking at it. I told the trustees that if need be I would pay the money myself. They told me they could afford it better than I but they didn't feel they should pay it. They were right and the insurance company was right. This was a situation that was covered in the document by stating very clearly that the only insurance payable was that in-force. That provision covered this precise situation of the limbo period between application and issue, or in this case, the signing of the application since that is all that would have been needed. It also covered the uninsurable situation, the rated situation, the employee who didn't want insurance, and the rest of the language which clearly defined payable or not. We were caught right in the middle of "what can happen, will happen," a la Murphey.

The amount of money was not large. The insurance in-force was $10,000 and the increase by formula was to $14,000, so at issue was $4,000. It seems even smaller as we talk about it in 1981 but it was bigger in 1966, and it's always bigger during times of strife, and most assuredly it's bigger when there is a question of "if" it is payable and "by whom."

I felt in my stomach that this claim should be paid. I knew legally there was no claim. Nothing could have been clearer than that. But there was no question in my mind that morally and ethically there was a heavy obligation to pay the money to this family. I decided to go to Tornoto and plead a good case to the proper department heads.

Recall, please, that it was December. I called the airlines and was told that because of the ice storm in our area all planes were grounded. I looked out of my window and although it was bad, the traffic was moving and I sold myself that the interstate highways were always well taken care of and I could drive without too much difficulty. The distance from Grand Rapids to Toronto was about 400 miles and in those days of 70 miles per hour, seven hours should have been sufficient to make the trip. It was about 11 am when I called the Royal York Hotel in Toronto and made a reservation for 10 pm that night. I was sure that ten or eleven hours driving time would have been sufficient.

The normal trip to Detroit would have been two hours and fifteen minutes but on that day it took five hours. It was still light and I figured if the rest of the trip was the same I would make the 10 pm arrival time. The weather suddenly turned worse. In addition to the ice already on the road, sleet started falling. I didn't know if I should continue or not.

I could have stayed at my parents house or I could have stayed in a hotel overnight and driven or flown the next day. But I had a mission in my mind and I didn't want to stop for any reason. I wanted to get to Toronto and get a good night's rest, if I could, to be ready for one of my biggest interviews ever. The weather got progressively worse. At times the visability was zero and I had to drive at three miles per hour. We were driving in caravan fashion, everyone being afraid to pass. If one car would have gone off the road, all of us would have. Everyone was afraid and edgy. I was tired and afraid of the skills of my fellow drivers.

The trip took all night and I arrived in Toronto at 8 am. A seven hour trip had taken twenty hours. I went to the home office and called the Royal York Hotel to tell them I had missed my appointment and to send the bill to my office. They explained to me there would be no bill and most of their guests had not arrived the night before because of the weather. I shaved in a bathroom, changed my shirt, and went to the office of Tom Walsh, the legal officer.

He was surprised to see me since we had spoken the day before and he felt the matter was closed. I looked terrible, obviously, and I must have been quite an apparition pleading a losing case. He listened and called Jack Wainwright, the chief claims officer, and asked him to come to his office. I went through the story again and they presented the perfectly correct legal aspect of the situation. After nearly an hour of conversation, they asked if I had any other business at the home office. I could see they wanted to be alone so I said I did, even though I had not one other thing on my mind. We made arrangements to meet after lunch.

I sweat it out until 12:30 when I promptly arrived at Tom's office. They explained all of the legal aspects to me once again. They put heavy emphasis on the fact that the client had been honorable people for many years and heavier emphasis on my convictions. On moral and ethical bases they decided to pay the claim. They asked if I preferred they write the claim check less the $230 premium or should the check be for the full $14,000 and collect the premium in the normal course when all of the new increases were issued. I chose the latter.

I left Tom's office and called the trustees. They were as happy as I and the pressure was off everyone. The client has been a valuable one ever since as they had been up to that time.

That was 1966. The story picks up again in June 1970. I had moved from Grand Rapids in January of 1970, back to Detroit and back into personal production. I was in my office when Ben's son called me and said he was considering the insurance business and had already interviewed with three insurance companies. He didn't want to be influenced by this story so he saw the other companies first before calling on The Canada Life. I had never met him before. When we talked I learned that the extra money in the claim check was helpful in allowing him to complete his education at Eastern Michigan University.

He did come into the insurance business with The Canada Life and has qualified for the Million Dollar Round Table every year since. This year Jerry Kaufman will be a Qualifying and Life Member. So the beat goes on. A small, proper investment of claim proceeds planted the seed and allowed a young man to enter the business and who was to place many millions of dollars worth of insurance in the hands of families over the coming ten years.

The story is intense enough to this point, but there are a couple of little sidelights, in addition.

Jerry's mother also worked for this corporation and retired in 1975. For years we had been pegging her retirement pension at a certain figure, but when she did retire and desired the annuity payments, the current annuity rates were higher than the guaranteed settlement option. She was able to have 15% more as a monthly income.

In addition, Jerry's brother-in-law, Neil Watnick, has entered the life insurance business within the last couple of years and we wish him the best.

Let us summarize this book and our great business by exemplifying all the positive things we all know with the motto, "Where Harmony Exists, Small Things Grow Great."

To summarize in as few words as possible, I use words effectively whenever I can. They sell! Proposals don't!! The businessman knows and appreciates this because his best automated machines won't do a thing without the brain of a man. I'm trying to develop an entire interview that I can do someday in just one word.

Glossary

Power words and their definitions

Will—note

Trust—bucket

Buy-sell agreement—umpire

Taxes—welfare and welfare costs

Cash Value—equity

Paid-Up Value—stop loss provision

P.S. 58 cost—P.S. 58 discount or tax shelter

Pension plan contribution—tax depreciation

Deferred compensation—exchange of promises

Term insurance—increasing premium; airline insurance or apartment rental

Permanent insurance—decreasing premium or land contract

Pension tax free growth—new math

Conversion privilege—rent with option to buy

One year term dividends—have your cake and eat it, too.

Medical examination—D & B report

Travelling examiner—he waits for you, not you for him.

Standard rate—prime rate

Pension enrollment forms and trusts—Marine Corps. applications—you'll be out in six years

Group insurance—no-fault policy

Rating—special premium

Issue or App delays—trying to get the best rate

Pension contribution—Monday's money

Waiver of premium rider—all meters going except premium

Filling out papers—exercise

Business insurance premium—wholesale cost

Permanent insurance for doctors—malpractice free savings account, creditor proof

Death benefit—beneficiary account

Accidental death benefit—full time flight insurance

Automatic premium loan—holding pattern

Low early cash values—"State laws require substantial penalty for premature withdrawal"

Optional settlements—budget

Annuity—reverse of insurance procedure—company pays you monthly premiums

Non-medical insurance—the company lets me put on my white coat for a few minutes.

Monthly check service or pre-authorized check—piggy bank savings

Participating policy—dividends, if any, paid to policyholder

Non-participating policy—dividends, if any, paid to stockholders

Monthly premium method—like the phone bill, one coming, one going

Paid additions—cost of living increase

Reinstatement—second chance

Family policy—group policy on same last name

Policy surrender—switch roles with company, you sell, they buy

Retired lives reserve—deductible limited payment life

Integrated plan—two-deck plan

Waiver of premium—premium holiday

Irrevocable trust—'til death do you part

Cash Value—owner's account

Face Value—beneficiary's account

Estate planning—social security for the rich

Flash Cards—see pages 64-69 for examples